Fall, Stand, and Repeat: My Martial Arts Journey

by Anthony Vano

Copyright 2017 Anthony Vano,

All rights reserved.

Published by eBookIt.com

ISBN-13: 978-1-4566-3039-3

No part of this book may be reproduced in any form or by any electronic or mechanical means including information storage and retrieval systems, without permission in writing from the author. The only exception is by a reviewer, who may quote short excerpts in a review.

*The book cover is a picture of me that my brother took after he saw the bruises I received from one of my marital art training sessions. I think the year was 2014. When I found this picture, I thought it would make a great book cover for my book. *

Table of Contents

Introduction 1

Chapter 1: My First Ninja Mission and My Introduction to Taekwondo 5

Chapter 2: Winning and Losing a Silver Medal 12

Chapter 3: My First Job at A&P, Jumping Rope, and Training Solo 21

Chapter 4: Oyama Karate: Osu 24

Chapter 5: The College Years: 1993–1998, The Five-Year Plan 32

Chapter 6: The Grasshopper and the Bartender 59

Chapter 7: Jeet Kune Do 64

Chapter 8: JKD Sparring 81

Chapter 9: Six Months' Severance: Climbing the ladder again 99

Chapter 10: Hitting Mitts 116

Chapter 11: Going to Vegas: The Martial Arts Hobbyist and the Real Fighters 124

Chapter 12: Haters, Bullies, and Fake People: The Sword and Shield Concept 133

Chapter 13: No Regrets—Thanks for Taking the Ride with Me 139

About Anthony Vano 144

Introduction

"Think lightly of yourself and deeply of the world."
—Miyamoto Musashi

This quotation sums up the way I think and approach my life as a martial artist.

This book will not teach you how to fight physically, but rather it's about Mentality. Through my story, you'll learn how my martial arts training gave me a powerful mental edge: a strong mind set. It's a book on how martial arts helped me on my personal journey—how martial arts helped me realize the power of respect, discipline, and honor. How important it is to control your focus and not let anger, frustration, or fear destroy you. Instead, use all of those emotions as fuel to push you forward. Turning that negative energy into productive action

I wanted to write a book on the trials and tribulations of my martial arts journey, from when I began at eight years old to my age now at 43. These are just my views. I'm not a martial arts expert. I don't own a school, and I'm not an MMA fighter. I'm just an average martial artist who enjoys learning and studying the benefits of martial arts. I had the honor of learning under many inspiring and amazing martial arts instructors. Along my journey, I learned a good martial arts teacher will teach you how to think, not what to think. The more I learn about training I realize it's about continuous refinement. That you have to dig deep inside of yourself and explore and face your fears.

This is just a simple story of an ordinary man who deeply enjoys growing and training in the martial arts. From my years of training, I developed a strong focus, a tested discipline, and a strong, positive mental attitude. Probably my best technique. The path of martial arts is not always easy. There will be times you will have struggles and disappointments in the dojo and out of the dojo. But through your training and a strong mental attitude, you will develop the perseverance to press on. A big take away for me from my training, one of many, many A-ha moments is that most of the time the attacker is not on the outside, but rather inside myself. Most of people's hard battles are fought in their heads. A SOLO BATTLE of you facing all your negative thoughts and if you're not careful you will become outnumbered . This is a constant battle for most of us, the inner war. However, the more you train, the more prudent you get to handle fear, doubt, or lack of confidence. How important the power of focus and goals are. Focus on the good not the bad. Run your head! Don't let it run you!

> "Some of the greatest battles will be fought within the silent chambers of your own soul."
> —Ezra Taft Benson.

Martial arts made me strong, like a one man wolf pack, **and not** to be a compliment junkie always seeking approval and validation. Instead, it taught me to have faith and trust in my skills. Martial arts gives me the **strength to conquer my obstacles and to take me to the next level. Remember there is always another level!**

All of these wonderful skills and gifts were all cultivated and developed from my studies in the various martial arts throughout my journey. I strongly feel if more people practiced and thought like a martial artist, the world would be a better place—where honor, bravery, and your word should mean something.

At this stage, my martial arts journey is primarily solo. I train on my own in my home. With my job and hours, it's hard to make the class where I used to train, and it's even harder to find a new school closer to my job. So, my home is my dojo. I find creative ways to train. I work on the collection of skills and tricks I picked up along my quest, and I work on developing them. It's constant practice and refinement. I also travel every year to the West Coast (California and Las Vegas) taking private lessons with different high-level martial artists and striking coaches. I've been doing it for the last 8 years. I absolutely love it. I research someone I always wanted to train with and find out the important details and location. Then, I book my trip and train for that lesson. I enjoy it so much! Just exploring and learning new things about martial arts and myself. There are no shortcuts while you climb the mountain. Step by step and slip and fall. There are no secrets, just dedication, hard work, and a desire to always be learning.

Lastly, this book has no martial arts politics or debates on what style is better. I wanted nothing to do with that. It's just an account of my journey from my perspective. Just a simple story about how the martial arts has been a beautiful distraction for me from the bull shit that life throws at me. Well maybe there is one secret I learned from all my martial arts training. And that secret is Fall/Stand/Repeat. Now begins my martial arts journey.

Chapter 1: My First Ninja Mission and My Introduction to Taekwondo

"Life code of a **ninja**: Never doubt, Never fear, Never over think"
—Unknown

In 1982, I was an eight-year-old boy living in New York. At that time, most kids my age wanted to be a GI Joe character, a Jedi, or a ninja. I wanted to be a ninja, big time! I got caught up in the ninja craze of the 80s: I had ninja pictures and posters all over my bedroom walls. Before I would go to bed, I would start to play make believe and create this secret ninja mission that I would have to complete. Fighting multiple attackers all alone with one goal in mind: to complete my mission at whatever cost. I would just get lost in my thoughts, visualizing myself in all black with my sword, throwing stars, and smoke bombs. The smoke bombs I'd use if I had to make a quick exit. I kid you not: if you'd asked me when I was a kid what I wanted to be when I grew up, I would have said a ninja.

One hot summer day, I decided to go on a real-life ninja mission and spy on my neighbor, Mr. Hopper. I created my own version of a ninja outfit. I proceeded to my backyard, fully committed to succeeding in my first mission, which I titled "Get

Intel on Mr. Hopper." I crept through the woods carefully so as not to make too much noise. I decided that I would climb a tree and set up shop up there. I could spy on Mr. Hopper and collect my data. You may be asking why Mr. Hopper. Well, Mr. Hopper was the grumpy guy in the neighborhood who would always yell and call the cops on all the kids: no one liked him.

I started to climb the tree with ease and confidence. I felt like a natural. I got high enough to where I could watch everything Mr. Hopper was doing. There I was, up in a tree, like a real ninja. I could see my target doing yard work in his backyard, smoking a pipe. I was close enough to smell the smoke. With my eagle vision, I was spying on everything Mr. Hopper was doing, mentally collecting data for my mission.

When I decided I had enough information for my case study of Mr. Hopper, I quietly started to climb down the tree like a highly trained ninja. However, there was a slight problem. This is where reality and fantasy collided. My fantasy ninja work was not in concert with reality. I was a short, fat kid who had climbed a tree way too high and now was stuck in it. I started to panic and made a lot of noise. I blew my cover, and Mr. Hopper spotted me. He stared at me in confusion. Mr. Hopper was now spying on me.

I painfully slid down the tree in embarrassment. I blew the ninja mission. Not to mention I was in extreme pain. To make matters worse, my ninja mask fell off as I was descending. When I finally crashed to the ground, I felt shame and pain. Shame that I didn't succeed in my first ninja mission and extreme pain from the scrapes I had all over my arms, stomach, and legs from sliding down the tree. I locked eyes by accident with Mr. Hopper. He just looked at me in disgust and pity and said, "What the hell are you doing?" I froze and said nothing. Mr. Hopper gave me one final look, then shook his head, wondering why I was up in a tree in the first place.

Mr. Hopper returned to his yard work. To my surprise, he didn't call the cops on me or tell my parents. Feeling defeated, I limped home. That was the end of my ninja career. Even with that botched mission, I wasn't derailed from martial arts. I had loved them from the very first time I watched kung fu movies on Saturdays as a little kid.

I have been a student of the martial arts since I was eight years old. I just turned forty-three, and martial arts is still an important part of my life. My passion continues to grow, and throughout the years, I have trained in different styles. Trained with gifted and talented martial artists and read many inspiring books on the martial arts that have helped changed my life, mind-set, and approach to how I deal with training and everyday life events. So, I decided to write a book on my martial arts journey. Why not? I'm just a regular dude who has a regular job. I'm no tough guy or badass black-belt fighter. When people ask me whether I'm good at martial arts, I say that I'm average. I've come to the conclusion that staying humble will keep you relevant and promote constant growth and improvement as a martial artist. From my martial arts journey, I've learned a lot of cool and valuable life lessons that have helped me throughout the years in all aspects of my life, and now I would like to share them.

I remember the night before my first Taekwondo class. I was so excited. I was eight years old. In bed, really late at night, I couldn't sleep. I just lay there, imagining what my first class would be like. I saw myself walk into the dojo, where all the students were doing backflips and jumping kicks to welcome me. So the next day finally came, and off I went in the car with my father to my first Taekwondo lesson. I was nervous, but I was ready to learn and build on my ninja skills. When I arrived, the instructor welcomed me and handed me a gi before pointing me to the dressing room to change. I can still smell the cotton of the new uniform. Before I entered the training hall, the instructor advised me to take off my shoes, that I was never to enter the room wearing shoes and that I must always bow before entering and exiting the training hall. He told me not to worry about putting on the belt, just to put on the pants and gi top.

I remember being in that dressing room all alone. Instinctively taking everything in, totally in the moment. When I came out of the dressing room, it was just me, the instructor, and a senior student. My dad waited for me in his car in the parking lot. I was wondering, where were all of the students who were supposed to be doing flying sidekicks and backflips to great me? I quickly forgot about it as I approached the head instructor, Mr. R.

He started to tie the white belt around my waist, showing me how to do it as he went. He then explained to me that when I addressed him, I was to say "Yes, sir" or "No, sir." He asked me whether I understood, and I said yeah. Mr. R quickly corrected me: "Yes, sir—not yeah." Again Mr. R asked, "Do you understand?" I replied, "Yes, sir."

Mr. R said, "Excellent." He then pointed to the top of the wall above the mirrors in the dojo and explained the ranking system. The belts went in this order: white, yellow, blue, orange, green, red, and then black. Mr. R explained to me that to be promoted to each belt, you had to take a test and pass. Next, he pointed to the senior instructor and told me she was going to teach me some kicks.

The first kick I learned was the front kick. The senior instructor had me grab the stretching bar and told me to pick up my knee and kick with my toes curled. So I could see, she showed me how to curl my toes as I kicked. She said, "If you don't kick with your toes curled when doing a front kick, you'll break them." She also showed me how to do the roundhouse and sidekick.

After that class, I was never the same. I had been bitten by the martial arts bug, and I've never recovered. It just felt so natural to me. Like I was made to be a martial artist. And for the next three years, I went to class every Monday, Wednesday, and Friday. I was learning kicks, punches, and forms. It was at this stage that I started to be able to focus on whatever task was at hand. To this very day, my focus is strong and productive thanks to my martial arts training.

I liked to spar as well as practice forms. I wasn't a gifted martial artist, but I had heart, and I was dedicated. I was a stocky kid who was solid. I was a sleeper; I had a basic sparring style. I enjoyed doing the roundhouse kick (back then, it was called a forty-five), front kick, and back kick. I never cried when I got hurt in sparring. It wasn't that I was tougher than anyone else. I just wouldn't lead on when I was hurt or scared. It was just who I was. I would spar the top students and instinctively check their kicks with my shin or knee, and they would cry. This technique came naturally to me. I didn't enjoy watching the top students cry. Just went with the flow, being in that moment. I clearly remember their parents, who were always watching them, look at me in total disgust after I sparred. The bottom line was that I held my own and took whatever was thrown at me. I wasn't as skilled as these top students, but I felt mentally stronger. My will was relentless. The meaning of sparring was much deeper for me. I couldn't comprehend or vocalize it back then, but I felt it. I had a strong, blind belief in myself.

All I wanted to do was continue training and growing as a martial artist. I didn't care about being in a certain clique; I just wanted to train. My parents raised me to be strong, and they were always supportive about anything I was passionate about. I grew up in a loving, extensive Italian family that always provided me with unconditional love and guidance. That alone fueled my confidence to bravely face whatever obstacle was put in my path or whatever goal I wanted to accomplish. My instructor took a liking to me, and every now and then, he would complement me in front of the class. I never liked being recognized in front of my peers and don't to this day. The attention makes me feel uncomfortable. Don't get me wrong—I like achieving goals, performing at my best, and being rewarded for it. Compliments are nice. But it still feels a little weird.

Chapter 2: Winning and Losing a Silver Medal

"I love those who can smile in trouble, who can gather strength from distress, and grow brave by reflection."
—Leonardo da Vinci

So as my training progressed, I got better. All I cared about was practicing and watching ninja movies. I was a happy kid. A big thing with Taekwondo was competing in tournaments and winning medals. I remember two brothers I trained with at the school. These kids were great, talented, and humble. They both had won many medals each, many of them gold. These cats were good. So, I wanted to take a stab at competing. I had already put in my work through sparring.

The first tournament I competed in, I had to fight a kid who was also a student at the Taekwondo school I attended. When the sparring match began, I was just going through the motions. I felt weird, competing at my first tournament with my first match being with someone I knew. My nerves got the best of me, and I lost that fight, but it didn't deter me. I went back to training and kept going to the school three times per week, and I practiced at home. I vowed that the next tournament I participated in, I would be more prepared. If I had to fight someone from my school, so be it.

When I attended my second tournament, I weighed 101 pounds, and I was ten years old. So here I am, this ten-year-old warrior sitting with a group of other warriors my age, getting ready to be called for battle. The day is moving . . . and I'm not fighting. Finally, the tournament is over . . . and I never fought? Then, one of the officials comes up to me and tells me the reason I didn't fight was that there were no ten-year-olds in my weight class. Epic moment for my self-esteem!

But here comes the funny part. Because there was no one else in my weight division, I technically advanced to the next tournament in Chicago, the 1984 Taekwondo Junior Olympics. Not the greatest way to qualify. However, both my parents and I saw it as an opportunity, and I was ready to take the ride. Even that young, I knew this was a rare chance to do something great in my life.

I had three months to prepare. I continued to go to class three times per week. Plus, my father set up a training program that he would do with me every night. I took this preparation very seriously. Of course, I was going to class every week, but what got me more prepared mentally and physically was the training my father gave me. He had me jump on milk crates in sets of ten, jump rope, and jog about every night. He put me in the mind-set that I needed to be ready for this tournament.

Back then, my dad was a mailman who also had a carpet cleaning business as a second source of income. So, my brother and I would help my father clean carpets on the weekends to save up for the trip to Chicago so that my parents, brother, and sister could come watch me compete. Years later, my father told me it had cost three grand to go to Chicago.

Thanks to my father's twelve-week training camp and going to Taekwondo classes weekly, I was prepared and focused. I had a lot of respect for my martial arts teacher at that time and for my father's wisdom and guidance. I was ready. I wasn't even scared. I know that sounds crazy, but I was far beyond driven. I was in peak mode. I felt like a ninja on a mission, representing my family and school.

The day finally came, and I arrived in Chicago with my family. We checked into the hotel, and then my pops and I went to the location where the tournament was being held. I weighed in at ninety pounds. They gave me an ID card and told us what time to show up the next day.

The next day, while I was at the tournament, they lined everyone up with other people from your state, and when your state was called, you walked out. I was very proud that I was repping New York. That November, my grandfather had passed away. I was close to him. I brought the mass card that had been given out when he died. I also had my grandmother's card who had passed when I was five years old. These were my father's parents. I put one mass card in each of my shin guards. I felt protected and powerful while I competed at the tournament under their watchful eyes.

I was sitting with a bunch of other warriors I had never met. We all were waiting to be called to go and fight. I didn't talk to anyone—any one of these dudes could be my opponent. I just stayed in the moment, taking it all in. Then, all of a sudden, some tournament official poked me on the shoulder and directed me to my instructor. It was my time to fight. My instructor helped me put on my chest protector and headgear. I remember my feet touching the gym floor. My instructor gave me a slap on my head and said good luck.

My first opponent and I squared off. I was waiting for the green, waiting to hear "go." When I did, I just set it off. I began my attack. Low roundhouse kicks with each leg followed by body punches. When the referee would break us up, I would throw a few lead sidekicks and an occasional back kick, then start back with low roundhouse kicks and body punches. The goal was to overwhelm my opponent with power and speed, and it was working. I had a very simple fighting style, and I still do.

Looking back on that moment, I felt special. I was relentless. I had true confidence thanks to what I had learned through training and sparring. At the moment, I had no fear. I fought my first opponent for two rounds, dominating both and winning the match. I remember my instructor being highly pleased and proud of me. After all, I was representing his school. It was a short-lived victory, though, because I went back to the bull pen to await my next match.

Again, I sat quietly observing and waiting for someone to tap me to tell me it was time to fight my next match. Just like that, I felt the tap on my shoulder. Everything went quiet, and I slowly stood and went into focus mode. It was the same routine: someone ushered me to my instructor again, and he helped me put on my chest protector and headgear again. I still had no fear. My instructor told me good luck again. I was ready. The entire gymnasium, full of people, made a roaring howl once I put my headgear on. Like when the wind blows and you're wearing a football or baseball helmet. All my senses were heightened. I locked eyes with my new opponent, and he had the same look as I did. And just like that, we heard "GO!"

We began to fight, and we both had the same fighting style, full of strong kicks and punches. I felt that I performed better, and I won that round. I noticed, while my opponent was sitting down in his corner waiting for the second round, that he was throwing up in a pail for whatever reason. To his credit, he came back to fight the second round, the last and final. I was quicker and more powerful. He had no gas left. I was declared the winner.

I remember after that match, while I was walking with my instructor, that I felt important. I remember that this big shot from Korea shook my hand and looked at the back of my uniform to see what school I belonged to. That moment stands out for me because it showed me how hard work and training paid off.

But I soon started to feel the pressure. I had advanced to the finals, and if I won my next match, I'd get a gold medal. Everyone from my school was there, and they were coming up to me and telling me I'd done a great job. I felt scared and nervous. The kid I was fighting seemed really tough and had a killer sidekick. I'd watched him fight earlier.

At that point, I didn't want to fight. I was cool with what I had already accomplished. But there was no way in hell that I would stop or quit just because I was scared. That is what is really amazing and special about the martial arts: it makes you confront things that scare you. When you face what scares you, you become stronger, confident, and enlightened. This feeling and experience can only be earned, never bought. So before my next fight, my instructor went over a technique on how to defend myself from a lead sidekick to the body. It was simple; he had me raise my knee to my elbow, and every time my opponent threw his sidekick, I would do this ramming technique to make his "money kick" less effective. It would also create an opportunity for me to close the distance between us and work my money game: low roundhouse kicks and body punches.

This opponent was tough and skilled. We were going back and forth. Every time he would hit me, I would hit him back harder. It was a battle of wills, and we both wanted to win. During the last round, I even knocked my opponent on his ass using the ram technique. I couldn't believe how much this technique made his sidekick less effective and weaker. It was a very close fight, and I felt that I had won. But they awarded him the gold medal.

I found out afterward that the referee of that fight was his instructor. Either way, it was a good fight. At ten years old, I had fought like a warrior. I had fought three tough kids for two rounds each, and I won a silver medal. I was proud. As I'm writing this, I'm looking at the picture of me raising my hand in triumph with the silver medal around my neck. What a feeling it gave me and my family back in 1984.

It still makes me proud. Three grand it had taken to fly my family to Chicago. My dad worked as a mailman and cleaned carpets—that's what paid for the trip. Hard work and sacrifice. Not to mention that if it hadn't been for my father's training and conditioning, both physical and mental, I never would have won at all. My instructor taught me techniques, how to kick and punch, and forms. However, my pops taught me heart and hard work. How to be consistent. He helped me develop my inner mental game and learn how to set and accomplish goals. How doing that begins in the mind. That moment for me on that podium, wearing that silver medal with my hands raised, was epic. Fighting three tough opponents in the same day! It was a life-changing moment for me and my self-esteem.

That moment has been a constant reference point for me in my life. When I go through difficult times, setbacks, or changes, I can easily pull that memory from the trophy case of my mind and gather strength and confidence. That moment has served me like a bright, soothing light that illuminates my journey when things are dark and cold.

I headed back home to a hero's welcome from my family. I was even featured in the local newspaper. The silver medal I won I leant to my instructor to display in the case in the school with all the other medals other students had won. My instructor had medals all over his office; it was impressive to see all those shiny medals. It looked like he had all champions at his school—not to mention that if you were a parent and wanted to enroll your kid there, seeing them would most likely impress you. A great marketing strategy.

I wish I could tell you that I stayed with Taekwondo and won many more medals, but that's not the case. Soon after I won the silver medal, my instructor seemed less and less interested in me as a student. I couldn't understand it, and it bothered me. I went from loving training to hating it. From being on the A team to feeling like a stranger. Someone who was in the way. I thought it was something I had done, and my confidence took a big hit. I went from hero to zero in a New York minute.

I realized as I got older that my instructor's behavior had all been a part of business. He went from kid to kid who had some talent, gave each one a lot of attention, had each one win a medal, displayed it in his office, and then moved on to another student. The day finally arrived when I told my parents I wanted to quit. They had a hard time understanding, but they always backed me up. I stopped going to Taekwondo class, and I never got my medal back. I left it there. At that point, I didn't even care about it. I just wanted out. He could keep the fucking medal. That was my mind-set. Looking back now, I regret not getting my medal before I left. But at least I have a picture that I can always look at to remind me of it. That silver medal is in my heart. I know how that sounds, but that's how I feel.

Years later, my mother told me that when I graduated high school, she sent my old Taekwondo instructor a letter asking for the medal and said that it was something that I should have as I got older. He wrote back saying that he'd lost it.

Chapter 3: My First Job at A&P, Jumping Rope, and Training Solo

*"I need to do things on my own,
need to be left **alone**."*
—Henry Rollins

I left Taekwondo when I was eleven years old. I thought that was it for martial arts for me. But as the years went on, I kept catching myself thinking about it. Whether it was watching a martial arts movie or reading *Black Belt magazine*, I honestly thought I would never practice or go to martial arts school again. But even before I realized how much I loved martial arts, it followed me like a hellhound. Fortunate enough for me, this persistent passion overshadowed the insecurities that were holding me back from training again. This drive, this calling, was written on my heart.

When I entered high school, I was a scared misfit. At fifteen, I started working at my local supermarket, A&P. Over the years, people have asked me, "So what high school sports did you play?" I would say, "Work." Their looks were usually bewildered and confused. Then, I would tell them that I worked throughout high school. Team A&P! During high school, I would work anywhere from twenty-five to thirty hours per week. I liked making money. I liked the freedom it gave me. I would go to school, go home, change, and go work my shift from four to seven.

It was at this time that I started to jump rope again just about every night. I became obsessed with it. I started doing it for one minute every night, and over the years, I was able to do more and more. At seventeen, I was jumping rope for twenty minutes straight with no skips. I would also practice roundhouse kicks and punches, often on a punching bag I bought with my own money from working. I hung it in my basement. It was a solitary escape for me. I enjoyed training and working out by myself. I was losing a lot of weight and becoming strong and fit. I still had the mind-set that my days as a martial artist were over. I didn't yet realize that the long hours of sweat and pain that I put into jumping rope were paying off. I was developing my footwork, cardio, rhythm, mental focus, and discipline. Religiously, every night, I would jump rope for twenty or twenty-five minutes and then work out on the used Bowflex machine that I purchased. Then off to the basement to work out on the bag, doing kicks and punches. Hitting that bag made me feel right; it made me feel safe. I was slowly developing strong roundhouse kicks and punches.

This was my life in high school: go to school, work, train, hang out with some friends on the weekends, and then repeat. These were some of the best times of my life. But there was something missing. This silent, roaring passion I had in my heart for the martial arts. I was still reading *Black Belt magazine*, and it kept me inspired and fed my thirst. It kept me informed on what was going on in the martial arts world. The pictures would motivate me. I would visualize myself becoming an excellent martial artist like the people I saw in the magazine. I would tape these pictures to my basement walls, right next to my punching bag. Little did I know that small area in the basement where I had the punching bag and martial arts pictures and posters was my own dojo.

My jump rope game was amazing: it became my ritual. I was up to thirty minutes straight with no skips. I would feel the burn in my legs, knees, and shoulders but wouldn't stop. I would keep on keeping on. I strongly believe that jumping rope has helped me with my mental discipline, helping me develop strong mental endurance and a tight mind. The sound of the rope hitting the rug put me in a deep trance, and I would focus on a better version of myself. I didn't realize it at the time, but jumping rope has given me so much. It was the connection of jumping rope and preparing for Chicago and winning that silver medal that was the formula for success that my father taught me early on, and it has changed my life for the better. By the time I started my junior year of high school, I looked like a different person after my growth spurt and working out. I was taller, leaner, and stronger. It felt good!

Chapter 4: Oyama Karate: Osu

"If someone asked me what a human being ought to devote the maximum of his life to, I would answer: training.
Train more than you sleep."
—Mas Oyama

During my junior year, a friend of mine kept telling me about the martial arts school he was going to. He was a black belt in Oyama karate. His school was named after the legend Mas Oyama. It taught the full-contact Japanese style of karate known as *Kyokushin*. This friend always told me to come and try a class. I thought about it, but I was intimidated to go. After a few months of thinking on it, especially while I was solo training, I decided to try a class. Right out of the gate, it was intense. As you entered the dojo—with no shoes, of course—you would bow and say, "OSU!" If you saw the sensei or fellow students, you would say, "Osu." If you were told something or a technique was explained to you, again you would reply with "Osu."

Some of you might be wondering what "osu" means. It means respect, to endure and strive to be the best you can be. I was really excited and scared at the same time. The last time I had been in a real dojo, I was eleven years old. But at seventeen, I was in the moment. Oyama karate was hardcore, nothing like Taekwondo. Even though I was intimidated, there was something inside me, pushing me along. When we did push-ups, we put most of our weight on our fists, focusing on the first two knuckles. It was painful, but it helped one develop strong fists and knuckles that would do major damage once they struck an opponent. I also learned to check kicks with my knees and shins. This was a cool moment for me because I remembered that I used to sometimes check kicks naturally while sparring in Taekwondo. That was a major game changer for me. Raising my front or rear leg with my shin or knee ready to crash into my opponent's leg, causing defeating pain.

To be clear, while training with your partner in the dojo, you never want to seriously hurt your training partner to the point he or she can't train. Always practice partner preservation. The goal is to develop and sharpen your skills in case you ever have to use them in a real self-defense situation. I also learned how to put more strength into my punches by practicing on taped phone books. Someone would hold one to his or her chest, and his or her training partner would punch with both hands over and over, with the emphasis on the first two knuckles. The entire class would count as one in Japanese from one to ten. It was powerful. What was even cooler was that sensei had a voice like Sato from *The Karate Kid 2*. Sensei would lead off the count in Japanese, and the class would say a number and then punch with total focus. Many times, my knuckles would begin to cut and bleed. But we were always encouraged to work through the pain and keep punching, to endure.

The day after class, I would have small circles of bruised flesh on the first two knuckles of each hand. It would hurt every time I would put my hand into my pocket to get my keys or wallet—not to mention the looks I would get from people, especially from my family, when they noticed. They thought I was off my rocker to inflict pain on myself and scar my hands like that. To be honest, I liked the reaction and the attention it brought me. I was proud of my scars and cuts. I worked through the pain and kept punching. To me, it showed heart and commitment. It was even harder to train the next day with knuckles that were sensitive and raw. They would reopen and bleed. Right after class, I would clean and pour peroxide on them to prevent infection. The goal was the more you punched the phone book or the makiwara (padded striking post), you would develop strong skin (less likely to cut) and razor-sharp knuckles that could open someone's flesh upon impact.

Most of the senior students had scarred knuckles. I even heard of crazy stories about how some Oyama karate martial artists went from striking taped phone books to hitting makiwara boards to starting to strike trees and rocks—talk about commitment to excellence in your chosen art! Now, I don't recommend that anyone hit trees or rocks. These were experienced martial artists who had put years into their training to condition their hands to be able to do that.

A lot of knowledge was thrown at me at once during this time. I was learning valuable skills that were changing me as a martial artist. I was also introduced to the hammer fist and taught how powerful the strike was. Constant drilling on low round kicks to your opponent's legs for sparring and low kicks to the knees for self-defense in the street. These skills and techniques are still part of my arsenal. To this day, I have strong hands and sharp knuckles ready to do damage if need be. Even when I do a fist bump to friends, they will say ouch and comment on how sharp my knuckles are. It's not like I'm trying to hurt them; it just happens because of what I learned at Oyama karate and the hours of training I put in there.

There was a pizza place I used to go to religiously and had since I was fourteen. Great New York Pizza. It was during Halloween that the restaurant had a really large pumpkin on top of the pizza counter on display. Every time I went there for a slice, I would eyeball the pumpkin and imagine punching a hole through it. I know it sounds nuts, but it was a goal of mine at that time. I'd think about it while eating a slice and sizing up the pumpkin.

After a week of going in there and studying this pumpkin, I decided to ask the pizza man, Joe, whether I could try to punch a hole through the pumpkin. He looked back at me puzzled and shut the oven door. He replied, "What? You botz!" That meant crazy. I responded, "No, really, Joe, can I punch it? Halloween is over, and I'll clean up any mess I make."

Joe looked back at me again, this time with a deeply concerned look in his eyes, and asked whether I was high. I looked at Joe, laughed out loud, and said, "No! I've been working on my punches through karate training."

Joe looked at me and finally said OK. It was just him and me in the pizza shop. He stood behind the pumpkin and told me to be careful. I began to clear my mind and control my breathing. I imagined my fist breaking the hard skin of the pumpkin. When I felt I was relaxed enough and had total focus, I counted down from three and threw my first punch with my right hand. Nothing happened, no break. Joe was pleading with me to stop, saying that I was going to break my hand. I assured him not to worry, that I had this.

Again, I cleared my mind the best I could and controlled my breathing. When I felt the time was right, I threw another punch, this time screaming, "KIA" (a power yell or battle cry). I broke through the pumpkin and was grabbing its guts. Joe was in shock. He looked at me in astonishment and said I had guts. That happened over fifteen years ago, and to this day, if you ask Joe about me, he will retell the pumpkin story with a heavy Italian accent. I was lucky I didn't break my hand. I don't recommend punching a pumpkin.

When it came to sparring at Oyama karate, I was nervous and unsure of myself. But there was this invisible, blind faith that kept me in autopilot, and it has never left me. The last time I'd sparred had been when I was a kid at my Taekwondo school. What's crazy is that I don't remember being that scared about sparring. Sure, maybe a few times. But the majority of the time, I didn't mind sparring class. However, the sparring I did at Oyama karate was as different as night and day from Taekwondo —when you would wear a chest protector, headgear, cup, shin guards, and hand guards. At Oyama, the only protection you were given consisted of shin guards, hand guards, and a cup. It was much more intense. Although you couldn't punch someone in the face, you could kick them in the face. It was scary, even more so because my confidence and belief in my martial arts skills was very low. I was distracted by my fear and doubt, strangling and choking my confidence. How was it that I had had so little fear and doubt when I sparred when I was ten? And how, at eighteen years old, was I scared while my mind went off in a million different directions? My mind was supposed to be empty, reacting and feeding off the moment. When I look back and examine those feelings and emotions, I think of this quotation by Robert Duvall: "When I knew nothing, I thought I could do anything."

But to my credit and warrior spirit, I would spar and for the most part hold my own. Nothing great but enough to where I wasn't taking a major ass-whooping in front of the whole class. One high point for me was after I had just finished sparring with a student who was twenty-five years old while I was eighteen. I remembered I was down on myself after the match. I was not impressed by my performance. I felt like I'd sucked. An older student, Lee, who was in his forties, came up to me and told me, "You're a natural at this, and you move very well." I was shocked to hear that because we are our own worst critics. Especially our self-talk. I so much needed to hear that positive feedback. Lee saw something in me that I didn't see in myself. That comment was like a life raft he threw to me because I was drowning in my own self-doubt.

That's the thing about martial arts. You're constantly learning how to deal with fear and stress, and I didn't realize it was normal and healthy to feel scared and apprehensive about sparring or getting hurt or looking bad in front of other students. Comparing myself sparring at ten years old and eighteen years old, it was two different worlds. Lee gave me a major confidence boost. He made me realize that I still had talent and heart for martial arts.

I stayed at Oyama karate for about a year and a half, my junior and half of my senior year of high school. But my heart just wasn't totally in it. I was slowly working my way back to a martial arts journey that I didn't even know I was on. I was running on blind faith. This drive I had was internal. As Mas Oyama says, "Come ye trials and challenges; come life's big waves, for I am ready." It's a constant reminder to always keep faith and to persist, to stand back up after you fall.

Chapter 5: The College Years: 1993–1998, The Five-Year Plan

"Man is a goal-seeking animal.
His life only has meaning if he is reaching
out and striving for his goals."
—Aristotle

It took me five years to earn my college degree—something I'm very proud of. The two moments that stand out for me in life are winning a silver medal in the martial arts and earning my college degree. I was the first in my family to do so, so it was a big deal to me. Not to mention how hard I had to work to achieve it. I barely made it out of high school. During my college years, my main focus was going to class and working. I didn't go away to college and live on campus. I went to a local college near my home. I would go to classes, and later on, I would go to work as a stock boy at A&P—the same grocery store I had been working at since I was fifteen. My workout and training consisted of jumping rope twenty to twenty-five minutes per night, doing rounds on my punching bag, push-ups, and some weight lifting.

Jumping rope was and still is a major part of my training. Even to this day, I jump rope three times per week. And it all started from that seed my father planted in my head while training me. Jumping rope developed my footwork and mental focus. I didn't realize that jumping rope was a full-body workout. When it came to jumping rope, I kept it simple. Put on some good music, set my timer, and begin to jump, shutting out the rest of the world. Nothing else mattered except jumping without breaking the flow. It's a total rush and release for me. A total mind and body connection. It kept me fit and continued to strengthen my persistence and faith. It fueled my fire and fed my passion. It also kept up my basic martial arts skills. Jumping rope was my compass that kept me on course on my martial arts journey.

A kid I went to high school with, Anthony, was a great martial artist. He studied traditional Taekwondo. Not only was he great as a martial artist, but he was also cool and down to earth. Over the years, I've met some great martial artists who had terrible and stuck-up personalities. Very cocky and treated other people badly. Very quick to devalue others' skills. But Anthony was different. He had real confidence as a martial artist and as a person. Real confidence versus false confidence—this would be a focal point I would think deeply about throughout my journey.

During that time, every now and then, I would hang out with Anthony, and he would give me some martial arts lessons. He would go over kicks and blocks with me. His traditional Taekwondo background had a hardcore style; the Taekwondo I had taken when I was kid had more of a commercial focus on winning tournaments. It was more about image and showing off medals and creating more student enrollment for the school than actual training and developing your spirit. Anthony's focus was more on self-defense, practicing forms, and sparring.

It was during one of our lessons that Anthony showed me a book called *Zen in the Martial Arts* by Joe Hyams. Anthony looked at me and said, "You need to buy this book ASAP!" I followed his instructions, and that day I bought the book and began to read it. This book changed my life as an aspiring martial artist. Reader, you need to go and buy this book—it's a game changer. I was introduced to it over twenty years ago, but I now have it in audio form and listen to it while driving. Some of the chapters in this epic book are titled "Empty Your Cup," "Know Your Limits," "Do Not Disturb," and "Make a Friend of Fear." The book is timeless and will help change you as a person and martial artist for the better.

During college, money was tight for me and especially my family. My life at that time was very disciplined. I was going to college, working at A&P, and training on my own. I read a lot of books on the martial arts and made myself a promise that I would join a martial arts school after I got my degree and landed my first gig out of college. That was a big focus for me. I thought about it all the time, even when classes got overwhelming and I was broke. I would just focus and dream of training at a martial arts school.

Thankfully, I never had to use my martial arts to defend myself. However, through training, without even knowing it, you kind of develop a sixth sense for trouble and danger. So throughout the years, I tried to stay out of trouble and not go to places where trouble lived and was always looking for a victim. I also believe that working a part-time job all through high school and college kept me out of trouble during those days. When my friends got in trouble for whatever reason, I was usually working.

Going back to how the martial arts have helped me develop a sixth sense. It gave me the ability to feel energy, both positive and negative, from other people. One moment that stands out in which my martial arts training kicked into autopilot was while I was working at A&P. A coworker was having an argument with someone who did not work at that supermarket. They began to argue in the backroom where I was taking a break, drinking an iced tea. The argument was escalating, and the guy who worked at A&P went into the deli connected to the backroom and came back with a long, sharp knife. He started yelling at the kid, flashing the knife. The other kid without the knife looked shocked and nervous but continued the argument with my coworker.

I started to panic. I had a front row seat to this horrible situation. These dudes were right in front of me, and it looked like something bad was going to happen. I slowly began to get up. My coworker with the deli knife made a motion to the other kid as if he was going to stab or slash him. I got up, jumped in, threw my forearm into his throat, and used my other hand to grab the wrist of his knife-wielding hand. I grabbed with all my strength until he released the knife and it fell to the floor. After the knife fell to the floor, the other kid ran out of the break room. I looked at my coworker and told him I was trying to help. That I didn't want him to stab the other kid. I don't remember what he said to me, but I do remember him looking back at me and nodding in silent agreement. I still remember the sound of the knife hitting the ground. The weird thing was that I just responded: my subconscious took over my body. My prior training automatically kicked in. It was a strange feeling. I wasn't trying to hurt the kid with the knife; I just didn't want to see something really bad happen right in front of my eyes.

I was lucky I wasn't stabbed or killed. A second too late or too soon and my life could have forever changed or ended. I had no knife defense training at that point. My Taekwondo and Oyama karate training made me react that way. Years later, I saw this quotation from Bruce Lee: "I do not hit. It hits all by itself." It makes me think of that moment when I reacted. It's made me thankful for my training and my never-ending martial arts quest.

Martial arts have also helped me set a game plan and focus on the target I want to reach. After seven years of working as a stock boy at A&P, I decided to quit and get another job. I wanted to go to bartending school and get a job at a local telemarketing firm. I was still in college and wanted to change it up, work less, and make more money while in school. So during the summer break, when I was completing my year of college, I quit the A&P. I worked at a telemarketing firm and went to bartending school on the weekends. I had this plan in my head, accomplishing the goals I set before they actually happened. This single-minded focus was like putting a GPS (navigation) on my goals. When I went to bartending school, I took it seriously, just like I had with martial arts. I studied and memorized all the drinks. When I would go out with my friends to bars, I would ask bartenders a lot of questions about the bar business. I gained a lot of insight into tending bar and advice on how to land a gig. It's amazing what you can learn just by listening. There is an art to it. Martial arts helped me develop effective listening.

When it came to training that summer, my favorite workout was punching and kicking my punching bag in my parents' basement. During those hot summer nights, sweating profusely, I would kick and punch my problems away. Sometimes, my mom would get upset because I would make the floors shake throughout the house. I was focused, obsessed with becoming a bartender. I wanted to accomplish this goal I had. After a month of bartending school, I graduated and received my bartending certificate. I was a certified mixologist in the State of New York. I was so proud. I had put the time and money into this. It cost me $300 to take the course. I was looking at the big picture, long term. The plan was to work a few nights every week as a bartender while going to college during the day. I saw myself working in a nightclub as a bartender, and that's what I did. I managed to get a gig at a multilevel club in Stamford, Connecticut. How I got this gig was the advice I received from a bartender.

One night at closing time at this local bar I would frequent, I was asking the bartender, Shawna, something. I was helping her put up chairs on the tables while my friends were playing pool. She started to break it down for me: the art of bartending. She was dropping gems, and I was taking it all in. One of the many things she told me was that if I was out and I saw a bartender who was in the weeds, overwhelmed and unable to keep up with the rush of the crowd, offer to help. That's what I did one night in this nightclub. I saw a bartender struggling, and I asked her whether she needed help. She said OK but asked the manager first. She pointed me to the manager. I approached this large man smoking a cigar. I explained I wanted to help the bartender, who was getting owned by the crowd. He said OK.

After I was finished helping, I was offered a chance to try out for a possible bartender gig. I was so excited that I landed a gig, and it kind of went to my head. I overestimated my passion and focus, and I underestimated that working live as a bartender was entirely different from imagining working as one. Sparring without headgear on. My first night as bartender, I was godawful, just horrible. I knew how to make drinks, having committed more than fifty drinks to memory, plus all the insight I had learned from talking to random bartenders. This was where my strategy failed. I didn't factor in what it took to work a live crowd as a solo bartender. It was extremely overwhelming. The crowd was evil. It felt like it was me against the world.

I remember I dropped my shaker, and when I bent down to get it, I didn't want to get back up to face the crowd. I thought the bartending game was not for me. But I got back up and faced the music, and I took my lumps. I was now in the weeds, and finally the owners sent a bartender to bail me out. At the end of the night, I felt so ashamed and defeated. I wanted nothing to do with this bartending hustle. I went up to the owner to give him my tip money. I didn't want it. I told him I was sorry for wasting his time. It was hard to look him in the eyes. I put the tips on the table and began to walk out. Then one of the owners yelled, "Wait!" I turned back around, and he said to me, "You're in. You showed crazy heart tonight. Most people would have run out of here, but you took the beating. You're in." He handed me back my tip money, plus my shift pay.

That was 1996. What a defining moment for me. How my strong spirit carried me through that tough moment. There is no doubt in my mind that my martial arts training, both physical and mental, helped me endure and face that fear and stick it out till the end. It made me strong. The never-ending pursuit of learning how to be comfortable being uncomfortable. A process that I'm still working on. Always trying to see the positive through the negative. Martial arts gave me a strong heart. I was extremely hard on myself my first night bartending. Thinking that being a recent graduate from bartending school with no experience, I was going to just crush it behind the bar—that it was going to be smooth sailing—was crazy. The fact that the first gig I landed as a bartender was at a multilevel club was impressive enough, especially considering that I had no bartending experience.

What's even crazier was that I got the guy who trained me at the bartending school a job there too. His name was Frankie. He told me how proud and impressed he was of me. I bartended at this place for two years while I was in college. During those two years, I felt like a rock star. It was like a cheap way of being famous. A shortcut to local fame. I'm proud of what I did. The strategy I implemented. How I set a goal, practiced and trained, and accomplished it. It all goes back to Chicago, to when I was a kid and won the silver medal. That was my fire. The key that opened the door for me and amplified my enthusiasm. My positive mental attitude, discipline, and dedication helped me. If I want something bad enough, if I put the work in, I can accomplish anything I put my mind to. Having real confidence in yourself is the ultimate rush.

Another defining moment that stands out for me when my martial arts training helped me occurred when I was in college. It was a Saturday night, and my friends dropped me off at the pizza place near my house, the same pizza place where I had destroyed the big pumpkin. I decided to end the night with a few slices. While eating this wonderful, mouthwatering pizza and drinking an iced tea, I was in my chill zone. Then, I realized a friend of mine was there, playing a video game. I said hello to him and went back to eating my pizza. He lived down the street from me. We weren't close, but I considered him a friend. There were three dudes sitting across from him while he was playing this video game. For whatever reason, they began to have words. I thought nothing about it because this kid was always getting in some sort of drama, but nothing usually ever happened. So I just kept focusing on eating this great pizza. Then, my friend broke my trance and told me that these guys wanted to fight him. He asked me, "You got my back?"

What could I say? I couldn't say no, and I knew there was a strong possibility that my friend started this altercation by being a wise-ass. He asked me again, "You got my back?" I just couldn't watch my friend get beaten up, and at this point, the three guys were already outside, looking through the window, waiting for us. Now I was involved. I slammed the crust of the pizza down on the plate and said, "Let's go."

I was silently protesting. I didn't want to do this, but I felt I had no choice. We went outside and faced these three dudes. I was desperately trying to be in the moment. I was scared, but I had to keep my head clear. We began to square off, and then all of sudden, my friend just turned around and ran. Our backs were facing a big hill, and he took off like a bat out of hell, running up this hill. I was in disbelief. The three of them and I began watching my pal run up this hill, and all I could think was that when my friend was no longer in eyesight, the focus would be shifted toward me. This intense moment finally arrived, and when I could no longer see my friend, I turned around and bravely (though I was scared shitless) faced these three dudes. They were just looking at me. I then realized they all had USMC shirts on. Holy shit! I couldn't believe it! I was seconds away from taking a major ass-whooping from Marines.

I was running on empty. The panic train was headed my way, full speed. I couldn't believe I was in this mess. And then out of nowhere, spur of the moment, I thought of something to say: "So is boot camp like *Full Metal Jacket*?" All three of them began to laugh. I began to speak from my heart and plead my case: "Gentlemen, there was no way I was running." And I truly meant that. I kept talking: "You saw what happened. I came in for a slice, my friend starts some shit, asks for help, and then runs?"

These marines were cool, very cool. And they didn't kick my ass, thank God. However, they had some choice words regarding my friend. These guys were true warriors. I told them I had much respect for the military and veterans. I like to think on some level they respected me for not running. Showing that I had heart, I wished them well and apologized for my friend's actions. I thanked them for not kicking my ass. I shook all three of their hands and never saw them again.

My martial arts training gave me the courage to face that moment and the quick cleverness to speak from the heart and to be witty and resourceful in a really stressful situation. I was disappointed at my friend for a long time, but after a while, I just dropped it, kicked it out of my mental wheelhouse. Everybody has their own reasons for doing what they do. The bottom line is I walked away from that situation unharmed. Even though I wasn't at a martial arts school, I still kept up with solo training at home and read as many martial arts books as I could. I couldn't wait to receive my college degree and land my first real job and then pursue my martial arts journey to earn my black belt. That's all I kept telling and thinking to myself.

During my junior year of college, my grandmother passed away. Growing up in a large family, both my Nan and grandfather were major positive influences in my life. They always encouraged me in all phases of my journey. How I miss those talks I would have with Nan at her kitchen table, which was converted into a full dining-room table for Sunday dinner. Powerful talks that inspired me to dream big. After she passed away, I got close to my grandfather. On Tuesday nights, I would go to his house and watch boxing. He was a tough dude who grew up during the Depression and was a WWII veteran. It was so cool to just hang out with him and watch the fights.

It was a tough time for him. He really missed my grandmother. But he kept it together for the sake of the family, especially for his grandchildren. He was the rock, the reference point for my entire family. He taught all of us how to live with honor and respect and how important family and faith are. My grandfather told me so many wonderful stories about growing up in the Bronx with his six brothers and one sister. How he never raised his hands at his older brothers. How much he respected and loved them. All his stories seem to have a valuable life lesson in them.

One story has stayed with me since he passed. I can't forget the look in his eyes and how serious he was when he told it to me. When he was a kid, he grew up in a very tough area of the Bronx during the Depression. Many times, he would have to fight to survive or to defend his honor or family. It was a hard life. There was this neighborhood bully who was bigger and stronger than my grandfather and would always pick fights with him. My grandfather would always accept any challenge and be ready to throw down. But according to my grandfather, the bully would always win the fight. But on one occasion, my grandfather's older brother happened to be on the same block when one of these fights was going to happen. Now my grandfather's older brother was watching this fight. When my grandfather realized his older brother was there watching him about to fight this bully, there was no way he wanted to lose in front of his brother. My grandfather won that fight and never had a problem with that bully again. I sit back and reflect on that story all the time. The love he had for his brother was deep and important, and that respect meant a lot to him. The potential fear and shame of losing in front of his brother was greater than the actual bully. That day, my grandfather was fighting for his family's name and honor. Talk about motivational factors.

My last year of college was really tough. I was taking six classes each semester. Money was also tight because I hardly worked—school took up most of my time. Thank God I was living at home. With the help of my family, I was able to survive financially and focus on my classes. I was blessed to have such a supportive and loving family. It was a grind; I still have my notepad from that time to remind me of assignments and tasks that I needed to complete. Every now and then, I will look through it as a reminder of my hard work toward achieving a dream.

In May 1998, I completed my last class and officially earned my college degree. It was a joyful moment for me. I remember going over my GPA with my guidance counselor, Al. My overall GPA was 2.8, and I told him I wished it was higher. He looked at me and gave me the greatest answer: "Your GPA is respectful, and ten years from now when you're mowing your lawn, it won't matter what your GPA was. All that will matter is that you have a college degree."

How right he was. Getting my college degree meant that all the hard work and sacrifice I put in paid off. And it was tight for my parents; they were paying for my college and my brother's college at the same time. It was a financial hardship for my family, but we fought through it. I will never forget walking on that stage and earning my degree.

After graduation, I took some time to just chill out and plot and plan. Not having to worry about the stress of school was so enjoyable. I took that summer off and started to actively look in September 1998. During that time, I worked as an on call custodian worker for a local school district. My dad got me the job. I even took a few police exams during that time. I wasn't too sure of what I wanted to do. But as always, I relied on the blind faith that I would land a good gig and make some money. I was still reading great martial arts books. Some of the books I was reading at that time were *The Karate Dojo* by Peter Urban, *The Unfettered Mind* by Takuan Soho, *Karate-Do: My Way of Life* by Gichin Funakoshi, and *The Book of the Five Rings* by Miyamoto Musashi. The more I read about the martial arts, especially the philosophy and psychology on training and life, the more I was just more focused and passionate. I couldn't wait to start my martial arts training again. Reading these books was training my mind and spirit by feeding it powerful wisdom and knowledge. My focus and mindset were getting stronger. It was a constant reminder of learning the power of real confidence and how it takes discipline to be positive all the time, especially during stressful situations. I would highlight important passages and later write them down on note cards. I would do that with all the books I read. Pretty soon, I had more than fifty note cards with different powerful quotes from different books. And throughout the day, when I had free time, I would read all these gems of knowledge over and over again to develop a stronger mind. I was and still am a driven individual.

I landed my first corporate job in February 1999—it was at an auto lending and collection company. During that time, my grandfather had just died from cancer. It was a tough time for everyone in my family. I was thankful I got close to him during that time after my grandmother passed away. I was hired as a temp employee with the possibility of permanent, full-time employment. I was hired as an auto collector for working in the collection department. I dove headfirst into this new adventure. It was a long first three months, but once I found out that I had been hired full-time, I began to start my search for martial arts schools to try out and see whether I vibed with them.

The first school I went to was a well-known karate school that taught its own style of martial arts. This school had two other martial arts schools in neighboring towns. My introductory lesson was with the sensei of the school. He welcomed me and was very nice. He asked about my prior training. Then we began the lesson. It was good. This sensei was good and showed me some great techniques. I was sold: I was the digging the vibe. So the next step was talking about price. Once he began to tell me the price, I was instantly turned off. It was $250 per month. The most I would pay was $100 per month. Remember, this was 1999. I thanked him for the lesson and said that I would need to think it over and would call in a couple of days with my decision. So that Monday, I called the sensei.

I told him that I wasn't interested. It was too much money. He then went into sales mode and started to apply these hardcore selling techniques to counter me. For example, he told me that I wasn't committed to and accountable for my goals. I just respectfully kept telling him no. He even tried to offer me a free gi if I would sign up. Again, I respectfully declined. I was thinking to myself, a free gi? This cat wasn't getting it. Paying $250 a month was crazy. Plus, he wanted me to sign a contract that would lock me in for a year.

The sensei was getting annoyed with me and how I stood firm with my decision, unfazed by his failed attempts to try to close the deal. Throughout the entire call, I maintained a firm, confident tone. I ended the call in a respectful and polite manner and advised the sensei that the price was not in my budget. He would call me once per month to see whether I'd changed my mind. After the sixth time, I advised him that I was not interested and to please stop calling me. He never called again.

I kept up with my search. I would go to different martial arts schools and would try a class at each. I wasn't a big fan of the politics of martial arts. I mean, it was ridiculous—some martial arts schools were like high school. Very superficial, follow the follower. If I saw or felt any of that, it would just turn me off of a school. I was looking to grow and expand my knowledge and wisdom and to become the best martial artist I could be.

One interesting story that stands out—I was doing an introduction class at a martial arts school that I was interested in. There was this black belt sitting cross-legged. She asked whether I could stand on each one of her legs so that she could get a full stretch to the point that both her knees would touch the floor behind her head. I politely said no because

I was afraid that I would hurt her. I was 250 pounds, after all. She got insulted and became angry. She snapped back at me: "I'm a black belt, your senior! I'm not asking you; I'm telling you." I said, "Yes, ma'am." I didn't want to make a bad impression. After all, this was my first class.

I slowly placed one foot on her right leg and then placed my other foot on the left leg. Within two seconds, she screamed at the top of her lungs to get off her. I got off her and asked whether she was OK. She didn't say anything and just waved me away with her hand to let me know I was dismissed. I never went back to that school either. I was getting frustrated; I hadn't thought it would be this hard to find a school. However, I didn't want to rush and jump into just any school either. Even extremely frustrated, I was willing to take my time and find something to help me grow.

After a few months of searching, I finally found a place I was willing to try. It was Goju-Ryu karate. I would train twice per week. The classes were held in a big gymnasium at a town rec center. At the beginning of class, we would run a few laps, then do some push-ups and sit-ups. After that warm-up, we would break into groups, advanced and beginners. I was in the beginners group. We would learn some kata forms and work on some kicks. Then, everybody would participate in controlled sparring, very light contact. I kept going to classes. I was so focused and committed to continuing my study and journey in the martial arts and, more important, to becoming a martial artist.

I was able to pick up a lot of the movements in the katas and kicks thanks to my prior training in Taekwondo and Oyama karate as well as my solo training. It was all coming together for me. A move that stands out from my short time training in Goju-Ryu was the eye rake, which I learned through a kata. It's a movement in which your fingers rake across your opponent's eye. At that point in my training, I'd never seen a technique like that. I thought it was cool, so I put it in my mental rolodex. A cool moment that stands out for me was when I broke two pieces of wood with a hammer fist. What a rush—I was proud! Breaking that wood represented the breaking of my fears and doubts. It was an amazing feeling.

One time, during controlled sparring, I was paired up with one of the senior black belts. He started going harder with the contact. I decided I would reply in kind; I thought it would be a good way to test myself. This black belt was good, strong, and fast. Yet I was holding my own. He was throwing powerful roundhouse kicks at me. I would check his kicks and fire back with my own round kick. I was also using good footwork, and he was getting angry at me. His face showed it. When the match was over, he was still annoyed with me. In my head I was thinking, I'd done nothing wrong. What was I going to do? Just allow this guy to tee off on me and take it?

I realized through my journey in the martial arts that a lot of those who practice have massive egos, which can hinder the way they teach classes, be students, or train with other people. Now, let's keep it real: we all have egos. But the problem with some martial artists with big egos is that they refuse to take any advice or feedback. And if you perform the technique better or just are a better martial artist, they shut down and have a mini meltdown. I feel this mindset will hurt you as a martial artist. You stop growing and evolving.

That senior black belt had the wrong attitude. The way he got mad over something like that . . . I didn't kick his ass; I just held my own. He decided that he was going to increase his power, and I did the same thing. I was this heavyset white belt, holding my own against a senior black belt. And over the years, through my training, I've come across some martial artists who are just full of themselves. The longer you have this attitude, the harder it is to lose it. And if you're not careful, your ego could end up in someone's trophy case. Some of these toxic martial artists can also be vindictive and try to sabotage you, especially if you're getting more attention than they are. They will try to diminish your skills. If I train with someone who is better than I am, I want that person to help me grow. I will ask advice about how can I do something better or what I am doing wrong. I will show that person respect and gratitude for giving me that needed feedback so that I can continue to grow as a martial artist. Like I said, I have an ego, and I'm competitive and like to win. However, I always try to keep my ego in check.

One of the many lessons I learned over the years with martial arts was to just train and try not to take yourself too seriously. Try to find a positive side to the situation. After all, martial arts training can be stressful if you're putting yourself in scary situations where you can get hurt or humiliated. Martial arts, for me, was a place where I faced my fears, whether it was through sparring with someone or doing a technique that could possibly hurt me or a move that I was uncomfortable doing. After doing something that scares you, after you face it and complete it, that's the greatest feeling ever.

While I was at the Goju-Ryu school, I met a really cool martial artist, Sensei Leo. Sometimes after class, we would talk about martial arts, and he would go deep. He was the first person I'd ever met who talked about applying meditation to the martial arts. I have read about meditation in the martial arts many times, but Sensei Leo was the first person to tell me he meditated. He said at night he would burn candles and meditate to clear his mind. He also talked about how he trained on his own. Sensei Leo would go to an empty field and practice different katas over and over again. In the hot sun, he would just spend hours perfecting his art. I remember him telling me he was just at total peace there, just himself alone with a gallon of water in an empty field. I thought that was so cool—to be totally self-involved in your craft. Sensei Leo talked about how he trained and the importance of eating good foods and drinking lots of water. He even taught martial arts free to kids whose parents could not afford it. This guy was cool, grounded, and real. That was the type of martial artist I wanted to become.

Sensei Leo was confident, and he was nice to people. But if need be, he could throw an ass-whooping on someone. I stayed at the school for about seven months. It was a cool experience, but it just wasn't doing it for me. It was time to move on. There were a lot of good instructors at that school, but Sensei Leo was the best, in my opinion. I moved on to another part of my martial arts journey. I needed something else. I thought seven months was enough time to see whether that school was for me, and it wasn't. It was kind of frustrating because I thought by then I would have found a martial arts school. I kept at my search and practiced at home. I felt like a wandering Ronin martial artist looking for my dojo.

To endure is one thing I have learned from martial arts, and that is what I did. I just kept solo training and continued reading whatever martial arts book caught my eye. The best takeaway I learned from Sensei Leo was the importance of keeping a journal and documenting your martial arts studies and training progress. This was great advice because then you will have your own success map to chart and can see how your progression is going in your chosen study. Sensei stressed to write to be honest and document what scares, frustrates, or annoys you while training. It can be a technique that is hard to understand and perform. He said to also document how you felt before, during, and after sparring. Journaling has helped me out big time in my training and in ordinary life. Stuff that was bothering me in the past is no longer an issue for me. It becomes a double pleasure to read old journal entries, raw and honest, as something that was bothering me. All these feelings are there on paper. It can remind you how far you have come and that you can get through and accomplish anything you put your mind and full effort into. As Benjamin Franklin said, "Energy and persistence conquer all things."

When looking for a martial arts school, you have to find what fits you. I recommend that if you want to join a school, try it out first and see whether you like it. Do some research on the school you're interested in. Read up on its style. Try not to make your decision based on one class; allow yourself time to think on it. And try many schools. Beware of martial arts schools that want you to sign a contract to lock you in for a certain period of time because if you decide to terminate the contract early, you will be hit with a big fee. I don't like schools that make you sign contracts. Most martial arts schools that are good and confident in their art and teaching don't have contracts. You pay on a monthly basis, and if you decide after two months that the school is not your thing, you can leave with no fee. Also, don't judge a school by the way it looks. The best schools I trained in were small; did not have the best equipment; and had cold, hard floors. The fancy schools that were big and super clean and had the best of everything were the worst schools that I ever trained in. It's just something to keep in mind. You should put the time in to research and find what will work for you. The Internet and social media are great and valuable tools. You can learn a lot in a short period of time. Back in the day when I was kid, there wasn't solid research like there is today, and you went to the school that was closest to your house.

Parents, you need to keep this in mind when you're trying to find a school for your kid: some schools like to do a lot of shows with their students. They will go to malls and fairs and put on demonstrations for the public. Some other schools are more traditional and just stick to martial arts and learning self-defense. I'm not saying one type of school is better than the other. But you as the parent know your kid. Some kids like to perform in front of people, and others don't. Also, be careful if a school tells you it will make your kid a black belt very quickly. Earning a black belt is a great feat, and in some styles, it takes almost ten years. Everyone learns based on his or her own abilities: it's not one-size-fits-all. It's an individual journey for each martial artist. Earning a black belt is just one of many beginnings of your martial arts studies. Don't get me wrong—it's a great accomplishment for a kid to earn a black belt, but the parent and instructor should advise the child that martial arts training never ends. I think this quote, author unknown, says it best: "A black belt is a white belt that never quits."

Another thing parents must do is never allow the instructor to be on the same level as you in your child's eyes: you're the parent, and this is the instructor. I see this happen a lot when parents shop with their kids. They go to the mall or supermarket, and they have their kid walking around in their karate outfit, showing the world that their kid trains in martial arts. I think that is a bad move. It could put a target on your kid's back. Instead of attracting positive attention, you're attracting negative attention. The wrong kid or kids can see that and look at it as a challenge and want to fight or hurt your kid. A simple solution is to bring a jacket or T-shirt for your kid to change into after class. Keep certain things a mystery to outsiders. Don't go into too much detail about your martial arts training. Just my opinion, folks.

At this point, my career was going well. I was on the fast track, and I had a super strong focus and desire to do well. I was still frustrated I hadn't found a martial arts school I could call home. But I still remained on my journey and kept up with my solo training. It was worth the wait. I just relied on my blind faith and knew it was just a matter of time before I'd find a school that I would connect with and find my flow. One year went by at my job, and I was promoted to a new position and got a brand new company car. It was an exciting time for me. I put the martial arts school search on the back burner and focused on my solo martial arts training and career.

Chapter 6: The Grasshopper and the Bartender

"Excuses are the nails used to build
a house of failure."
—Jim Rohn

In 2003, I decided I wanted to bartend again, which I hadn't done since the late nineties. I felt I had some unfinished business with bartending. I pulled out my dusty note cards with drink recipes on them and started to study the drinks and recommit them to memory. Thanks to my martial arts training, when there is something I want, I become fixated and obsessed with achieving it. I start to analyze the goal I want to accomplish. It's like whatever goal I focus on becomes 3-D to me, and I focus on it from all angles. I look for doors and solutions that will help me along my journey.

Sometimes it takes me a long time to achieve my goals. I view goal setting and learning as forms of transportation. Some people take a plane, train, car, or go horseback, walk, or even crawl in pursuit of their goals. I take a train to California. Once my heart and ability connect and meet, I'm at my best, in peak mode. So, my focus was strong to get back to bartending. My career at my first job was going great. While driving, I would pass this catering hall that had a castle-like presence. It was quite magnificent. For some reason, I would tell myself that I would work there as a bartender one day. I don't know why I was saying it, but I just felt it. I kept studying new and old drink recipes and committed them to memory. When I felt I was ready to bartend, I went to the catering hall and filled out an application. I put all my bartending experience on the job application. After I filled it out, I handled it in and left it to chance. The next week, I got a phone call that my first day of work would be Saturday, July 4. I was excited and had driven by this place a hundred times, and now I was getting an opportunity to bartend there.

July 4 arrived. I was still living at home with my parents, and as always, they were very supportive with anything I wanted to do. I had to wear a tuxedo shirt, black vest, and bow tie with black pants. I must say I looked sharp. I was nervous. I hadn't bartended in almost five years. I walked in the catering hall and met the head bartender, Sam. Sam showed me around the establishment, giving me the layout of all the different rooms and bars. Then out of nowhere, Sam asked me, "So what bartending experience do you have?" I said I'd worked in a nightclub, and Sam just nodded. Then I confidently said, "By the way, I went to bartending school." Sam looked at me and said, "It means absolutely nothing you went to bartering school, and I recommend you don't volunteer that information here."

Sam continued his verbal beat down of me. "Bartending experience is what counts; that's what I'm looking for." I looked at Sam right in the eye and said OK. I understood. I think most people would have been intimidated by the first encounter I had with Sam or even insulted, but I wasn't. From my martial arts training, I have learned to develop a quick eye and look deeply into all matters. I saw that Sam was willing to give me a shot, but I had to earn it. Sam pulled no punches with me. He made it very clear what he thought of bartending school. He also wanted to see whether I had thick skin, and through my training and reading, I developed the attitude to never expect gratitude so I could never be disappointed.

My first gig was with Sam and two other bartenders. It was a big wedding of more than 200 people. I had a lot of fun and did pretty well. Sam was impressed with my bartending game and put in a good word for me. I started working every weekend, doing doubles on Saturday and sometimes on Sunday. I felt I finally connected as a bartender. It was very different from when I worked in the nightclub. I really lucked out when I landed this gig. I was around so many experienced bartenders who were willing to share their knowledge with me. Again, it was my quick eye that I developed through martial arts that made me pay close attention to the signs and opportunities that were placed before me and helped me have a grateful attitude. I would constantly remind myself that I was a banquet bartender for a very popular catering hall. I was flooded with so much joy and pride. I had gone back to bartending and done well, very well.

I also had a great rapport with the guests at the weddings. Everything fell into place for me as a bartender. That was 2003, and I proudly worked at the same catering hall for ten years. What started out as an idea and plan to become a bartender was what I accomplished with the strong, single-minded focus I had learned through martial arts. A strong, tight mind that blocked out all the negativity and doubts. I didn't care what anyone thought or said, and I still don't. When I want something bad enough, I keep it in my wheelhouse till I reach it or feel satisfied with the outcome of the goal I desire.

I'm very careful with deadlines for goals. I think what is important is to stay on your journey. My mom used to have this magnet that she put on the fridge that said, "Don't wallow in self-pity." I'll admit I get down and frustrated when things don't go my way or something that I'm really working hard at doesn't work out. Especially when it seems like you're working really hard on not achieving the desired goal you seek, such as losing weight. You follow a good diet plan, and you're working out. Then, you weigh yourself, and you've gained weight instead of lost it. That is extreme frustration. Real anger. Working hard and getting poor results. I get mad and will stay mad for a few hours and sometimes a few days. But I always go back to what my mom had on the fridge: "Don't wallow in self-pity."

From the martial arts, I developed a strong warrior spirit and mindset to never surrender. To never give up on myself and always believe. To have a positive mental attitude. A powerful mind that will shield me from all negativity. All the poisonous arrows that will try to damage my spirit. I confidently defend and constantly seek inspiration that will fuel me on my martial arts journey.

Chapter 7: Jeet Kune Do

"You can never invite the wind, but you must leave the window open."
—Bruce Lee

When you least expect something to happen, it does. On one Saturday night in 2005, after being at a bar with my good friend Dave, we were going to get something to eat when we made a wrong turn and ended up in this business complex. I saw this sign that said Jeet Kune Do. I told Dave, "STOP!" I got out of the car and ran up to the sign. It was glowing and calling to me, late at night. I was just bugging out on the sign. I asked Dave for a pen and wrote down the phone number. When I got back in the car, Dave was looking at me like I was nuts.

"What was that all about?" he asked. I explained to him that the martial arts school looked interesting to me, and I was going to check it out. I was downplaying my excitement. Inside, I was fired up. It was like beautiful fireworks going off inside me. That Monday, I called the school and spoke with some guy who said I could try out a class for free. I inquired who I should ask for. The man said Sifu. I said OK, and the countdown began.

The school was forty-five minutes from my apartment. I finally had my own place. I remember being in the lobby before meeting Sifu. The door of the dojo was shut, and the windows were blocked by curtains. All I could hear was music playing and people talking. Every now and then, I would hear a crash, as if someone had just been thrown into the wall. BOOM! BOOM! The pictures in the waiting room would shake. It was intimidating, especially given the fact that I couldn't see anything, only hear. My imagination was running wild. I remember sitting there in the waiting area, being so anxious and excited. I was looking at the Bruce Lee pictures that were hanging. I sat in silence, alone with my thoughts, in the moment. I was the only one in the waiting area.

Suddenly, the music stopped, and I heard a brief silence before clapping. What the hell was going on in there? The window that was blocked by the curtain was now pulled back, and I could see some of the students looking at me, not mean-mugging me, just looking. Then the door opened, and I saw a man dressed in black. He looked at me and said, "You must be Anthony." I said, "Yes, sir," and I extended my hand. He shook it and said to come on in.

As soon as I walked through that door and entered that dojo, my life changed as a martial artist. Two words that came to my mind when I met Sifu were "calm" and "cool." He had this calmness and confidence that were quite evident. I had major sensory overload: so much was going on. The first thing Sifu said to me was that jeet kune do means "the way of the intercepting fist" and explained it was Bruce Lee's art, designed for self-defense in the streets. He told me that you're in competition with no one but yourself. I was getting quite familiar with that feeling of being the new kid in the dojo. After all, I had been trying to find a school since I graduated college—five years on and off of visiting different martial arts schools.

The students had on sweatpants and T-shirts, and they were wearing sneakers. I noticed a message on the floor that said, "No street shoes." You had to wear sneakers that were meant only for training. While I was talking to Sifu, he had me sign a waiver that if I got hurt or killed, he and the school were not responsible. WOW, I thought. I had never had to sign anything like that before, but I did it. There was something special about that school. I could feel it. Like I said before, I had major sensory overload my first day at this school. I was in this large room with cold, hard floors and a damp smell. There were mirrors on one side of the dojo, and all the students could see themselves working out. At the end of the room, there were all types of training equipment neatly organized. Focus pads, headgear, chest protectors, and hand gloves. On one wall, there were pictures and autographs of famous martial artists that Sifu had trained with. Most of the students were quiet but seemed friendly.

Sifu pointed across the room and advised me to grab a jump rope, that the class started with jumping rope. My eyes lit up like a Christmas tree. I couldn't wait to showcase my skills in jumping rope. After all, I had been jumping rope religiously for the last eight years. Jumping rope was my martial art. I walked down to where all the jump ropes were. I went through all the ropes to find one that suited me. I couldn't find one; they were all too short. I finally grabbed a rope that I thought would work for me. Then, Sifu commanded the class to jump rope. He put music on.

Here was my moment. I thought of all the times I'd jumped rope throughout the years, sometimes for thirty minutes straight. Countless hours I'd put in. I will definitely make a great first impression, I thought. I felt so confident. When I started to jump, I couldn't find my rhythm; the rope was too short, and I kept skipping. Are you fucking kidding me, I thought to myself. I was getting so frustrated and looked so foolish. It looked like I had never even picked up a jump rope in my life. I started to laugh at myself; I didn't want this little problem to overshadow my focus and attention. After all, this was my first class, and I had learned a good lesson: it's not good to show off. I also made a mental note to bring my own damn rope next time.

What really impressed me about that school was how students could ask challenging questions about the technique that was being covered. Other martial arts schools that I had attended over the years did not allow that. It was their way or the highway. Follow the follower. However, at this JKD school, free thinking was encouraged. Another thing that freaked me out was the music that was played during the class. All kinds of music: rock, hardcore metal, rap, and jazz music. This school had a calming atmosphere, and the focus was strong, super strong. All the students and Sifu were laid-back. However, at the same time, they all had an extreme sense of urgency. A deep desire to learn and get the most out of each class. The auras and vibes of all the JKD practitioners were impressive and intense. I had never seen a school like this. I had finally found my home, my dojo.

I was paired up with another student named Chuck. He was very helpful with any questions I had. The first technique we did was called a low hook kick (low roundhouse kick). Chuck would hold a focus mitt at waist level and explain to me, while I was kicking my target, that I should aim for my opponent's knee or groin. Chuck then asked me whether I was a righty or a lefty. I said righty. Chuck explained that in jeet kune do, we put our power side forward. So instead of having my fighting stance with my right leg in the back, I would put it forward. That is how JKD martial artists fight. Your strongest weapons are put forward, closer to your opponent's vital areas.

So, I went from being trained all these years to fight with my power side in the back to changing to doing the opposite. I was confused, but I went with it. I trusted what was being said to me. This school was different but in a good way. Chuck asked me whether I had trained before. I said a little. Chuck replied, "I could tell—you have power in your kick." It felt good to hear a compliment, especially on my first day.

While on your martial arts journey, you won't hear many compliments while training, so be thankful and show gratitude when you do. Then move on. Always move on. Don't become a compliment junkie. Compliments are rare and earned, especially in martial arts. They should also have a short shelf life. Never be bound by compliments. Never let them go to your head. Beware of schools that give too many compliments; they may not be genuine. This also could breed false confidence in a martial artist. In my opinion, the goal of the martial artist is to always train and grow. There is always room for improvement. If anything, use the compliments as fuel to train even harder. I have seen many martial artists allow compliments to go to their heads, and they get full of themselves. A direct result of this toxic thinking is that they stop growing as martial artists. They kill off and destroy their own potential.

In your martial arts journey, you will have more constructive criticism than praise. Also, know the difference between constructive criticism and haters who just put you down and make you feel inferior as a martial artist. No one should tolerate that, but I will keep it real with you. As I stated earlier, there are many big egos in martial arts, and sometimes these creeps will make other martial artists feel like they suck. They may try to put you down or constantly correct you to play mind games. It can be very trying and intimidating. I have dealt with and even been paired up with many energy vampires like this, and it just makes your training sessions lousy and unproductive. How I deal with these toxic people is to just yes them to death and try very hard to limit my training with them. Everybody goes through it, and you just have to find a way to deal with it.

Now going back to constructive criticism: sometimes we don't want to be corrected because we allow our egos to get in the way. It still happens to me from time to time, especially when I have someone twenty years younger than I am giving me advice. There are many times I would dismiss it because I allowed my ego to be the boss. Some of the advice these young martial artists were giving me was very valuable. For example, one student advised me that he could tell before I would throw my lead hook kick. He stated that my fingers would to start move. It meant I was telegraphing my plan of attack and my opponent could have an advantage over me. When I started to listen and correct my mistakes, I did better in sparring and overall as a martial artist. There will be people along your journey who want to help you improve and grow as a martial artist. Welcome and thank them for their feedback. This quotation by Norman Vincent Peale helps illustrate my point: "The trouble with most of us is that we would rather be ruined by praise than saved by criticism."

Mondays and Fridays were when I went to class. Each class was better than the last. What a great way to start and end my workweek. I was excited to go to each class, like when I was kid on Christmas morning. The excitement of the unknown, not knowing what I would get. Each time I left class, I was better than I had been when I walked in. When Sifu taught class, it was always amazing—the way he explained techniques and the way he would teach and coach the students. The lectures he would give and how he would break them down. The points he tried to make were an art themselves. There was always good music playing to get you pumped up while you were training, and it would make what was covered more memorable. I was dialed in, committed, and focused. Each time I left class, I would write in my journal what I had learned, who had taught class, and whom I had trained with. I would also include random thoughts about how I was feeling when I was doing the techniques and my overall performance for that class. Keeping a journal and documenting most of the classes have helped me big time in my martial arts training and in writing this book. From reviewing my journal, I can track my progress and see areas where I can grow, which I call OFD for "opportunities for development." I also use the journal as a reminder of how far I have come as a martial artist and person. Thanks to Mr. Leo from the Goju-Ryu school for giving me the idea to start journaling my martial arts journey.

When you have a good instructor, you will have good students. Sifu set the benchmark high by being a great martial artist and amazing teacher. His students wanted to emulate him. To have those solid qualities: strong eye contact, a light smile, deep focus, and a strong commitment to training and growing as an individual and martial artist. With a fresh mind, I would go to each class, eager to learn and grow. As the famous quotation says, "Empty your cup." I took all my former training and techniques and mentally shelved them. I didn't abandon them; I just put them away so that my mind was open and not bound by my previous training. I wanted to learn new skills, and with JKD, I was learning so much.

For example, I learned that when you punch, you use a vertical fist, even when you throw a hook punch. I also learned that 90 percent of your strikes are from the lead hand and 10 percent from the rear hand. I also learned to block and parry with the rear hand. The lead hand is the sword, and the rear hand is the shield. I would partner up with someone, and we would take turns holding the focus pad. When it was my turn to hit the focus pad, I would hit hard. I loved the sound my fist made when I struck. My punch would make such a loud slap and pop. That sound became my focal point. Instinctually, I knew I was striking correctly if I heard that sound.

The feedback I got from my training partners was also motivating. They would say, "You got power, and you're fast for a big guy." It was nice to hear. But again, I never allowed it to go to my head. Training was deeper for me. It was primal. It wasn't like I was trying to show off, not at all. It was just that I took the training seriously to make up for lost time. All those years training alone were paying off now.

Extreme joy and gratitude flooded me. I started to bring my own jump rope, and before class, all the students would jump for about three minutes straight. I would make it a silent competition to be the only student to jump the three minutes straight with no skips, and I always succeeded. I ran the jump rope at the school when it came to straight-up endurance. I took great pride in jumping rope. It made me a better martial artist. It gave me an edge with my footwork and physical and mental endurance. I felt like an artist with that rope.

I also learned about economy of motion at the school. Not to make excess motions or telegraph your punches or kicks. Not to draw back and to be flawless in executing your technique. In my prior training, when I learned something, I just took it at face value and practiced it till I was able to do it with confidence. But now, because of my jeet kune do training, I was becoming more of a cerebral martial artist. I knew to pull back the curtain and investigate and explore the technique or theory to get to the core of it. I learned a wealth of information quickly, including how important the lead side kick was. The longest weapon to reach the nearest target. The rolling back fist (low and high) and the elusive lead. How to use the elbows and forearms against body shots. It was a beautiful time for me as a martial artist. I was thriving, focused, and driven.

Before I knew it, I was told I would be testing for the next phase of my JKD training. I was in phase one for nine months, and it flew it by. What I learned in those nine months was simply astonishing. Before JKD, my approach to martial arts had been that you needed a good ABC game. But I realized to be an effective martial artist, you needed a solid A-to-Z game regarding self-defense. JKD made me shift my focus and look at martial arts as a way to protect myself from being attacked on the street, in the parking lot, or in elevator. To look at it not as a sport, a competition, or a means to getting a certain rank or belt. The test for phase 2 of JKD training was tough, and I was nervous. I had to know a combination of strikes and kicks, correctly parry and block, and know some JKD terminology. The test lasted almost two hours, and I was with six other students who were also testing.

After the test, Sifu called each of us to the center of the room and told us all whether we'd passed or failed. There were two students who did not pass, and Sifu advised them that they would have a chance to retake the test in two months. Sifu then called me to the center of the floor and told me I'd passed. I was so happy and proud. I was now able to take advanced classes and train more. I was training three times per week, sometimes four.

I will never forget the first day I went to phase two training. What was being taught was on another level. I was intimidated. There were also seniors in these classes I'd never seen before. Some of the students who were promoted with me were at the class, so it felt good to see familiar faces. Sifu introduced us to the phase two class and said that this was our first advanced class. The first technique Sifu taught us was the headbutt. This blew my mind. I was in shock. I was going to learn how to do a headbutt correctly. Sifu explained that the way the headbutt was shown in the movies was incorrect. This whole JKD experience was so much more than I had expected. I was learning some high-level stuff. Just watching Sifu perform this technique showed how devastating it could be, and it was chilling and remarkable at the same time, beautiful violence.

Sifu said the headbutt was the ultimate equalizer when dealing with an overwhelming attacker or attacker with a weapon. He also made it very clear not to show or teach people the techniques that we were learning. "Keep it to yourself," he said in a very serious tone. We earned and paid our dues to learn this art. It made a lot of sense to me what Sifu was saying. I could show someone a move I learned, such as the headbutt, and down the road that person could use it against me or for the wrong reason and hurt someone. I learned early on in my martial arts journey to listen more and talk less. Be a mystery to your opponents. Keep them guessing, in suspense. My mindset on martial arts was changing completely.

Before JKD, my big focus was to get a black belt; I was rank driven. Doing JKD completely changed that: becoming a black belt was no longer a focal point. I just wanted to train and grow, to practice over and over again to master the basics. The more I trained, the more I realized how little I knew. When you train in the martial arts, it's a constant quest for improvement. I was in peak mode on my JKD journey between going to phase two classes and learning new stuff and going to phase one to relearn previous material.

I was learning new footwork, how to move gracefully and be elusive—moving forward, backward, and sideways while maintaining a solid fighting stance. Sifu would stress to the class how critical and extremely important footwork was. He would say to never cross your feet while sparring or fighting because it would set you off balance and make it easy for your opponent to take you to the ground. It was difficult and challenging to learn this new footwork; it was like learning a new way to walk. But I was picking it up quickly. I had a slight advantage thanks to my jumping rope.

The first six weeks of phase 2 training, Sifu covered footwork. I was learning the step and slide, pendulum step, and pivot. Some students were getting frustrated with all the footwork. They wanted to learn other things such as punching, kicking, hitting focus mitts, and kicking kicking shields. It didn't bother me at all because I knew how important footwork was. I started to move well. "Very elusive," some fellow students would say, or, "You move well." But I knew it was not by accident or natural ability. I forged my ability to do footwork from the countless hours I spent jumping rope over the years. Hard work, commitment, and discipline. I was trying to put it all together, learning how to apply footwork to help my punching and kicking. I would do a lot at home too, doing my version of shadow-boxing, incorporating footwork. I was working on my JKD craft. I can honestly say that JKD birthed my style as a martial artist. I didn't care how long it took or how foolish or clumsy I looked at times while training. All I cared about was training and learning some deep insight into and philosophy about martial arts and life. I was on my quest, my journey to be the best martial artist I could be. And I still am.

I was exploring new lands. Sifu started to cover trapping, which I knew nothing about. Hand immobilization attacks—this was completely new to me. Some techniques we covered were pak sao (slapping hand) and lap sao (grabbing hand). The purpose of the trap was to hit. There should be a hit before and after every trap. Trapping was and still is a new world to me. These were good times for me as a martial artist. This is what I had been searching for all those years. As I advanced in my training, I would at times leave class frustrated because it was hard for me to grasp the technique and comprehend it. Like most of us, I am my own worst critic. But through my constant training, I learned to embrace that frustration and just be patient. This frustration was a way my subconscious was telling me that I had information overload and needed to chill.

I learned to let the technique find me, to stop forcing and rushing myself. This approach has helped me greatly in my training and in my life. Sifu was dropping knowledge left and right. Each time I left class, I left as a better martial artist in skill and knowledge. Words can't describe it. I waited my entire life trying out different schools, reading countless books describing in detail martial arts instructors like Sifu. A teacher, sage, and great fighter. I had found a martial arts school that accepted me for who I was. I had found a martial arts teacher without a big ego. I had found a down-to-earth martial artist who wanted to teach self-defense to his students and a school that welcomed individuals who thought freely and were not followers.

I was also learning ranges of fighting: long, middle, and close. I grew to understand that long range is good for kicking and that when you're in long range, you should be relaxed to conserve your energy. Middle range is good for punching and at times trapping, and in close range (the danger zone), you use headbutts, your knees, your elbows, and grappling. When you're in close range, you need to turn it up and go all out because you're subjected to dangerous strikes and your opponent's bad intentions. I also learned about the primary targets: eyes, throat, groin, knees, and ears. You could use an ear slap (palm hook) in close-range fighting. Sifu also taught us how to feint while striking. I was leveling up as a martial artist and starting to realize that if you don't practice what you learn on a weekly basis, you can lose it. It's like a plant: if you don't give it light, attention, and water, it will die. The skills you develop from training need constant attention, or you will lose your edge as a martial artist. Your skills will perish if they don't get proper attention and devotion.

Sometimes it was hard to empty my cup from my prior martial arts training. For example, when learning how to do the vertical punch, you aim with the three bottom knuckles. This was a work in progress for me. In my prior training, I had learned to hit with my first two knuckles, and now I was learning a different way. It was frustrating. However, after a while, I looked at it like this: I would have the best of both worlds. I could already hit with confidence using my first two knuckles. Now, I would learn to strike with power when doing a vertical punch to hit with the bottom three knuckles. Problem solved—another example of how a good attitude helps everything in life.

I also started to read *The Tao of Jeet Kune Do* by Bruce Lee. Reading this book while training in JKD was epic for me as a martial artist. I strongly recommend it. It's another game changer. What a great man, great martial artist, and philosopher. Bruce Lee changed martial arts and the world for the better.

Chapter 8: JKD Sparring

"Fear makes the wolf bigger than he is."
—German Proverb

The first time I saw JKD sparring, I was terrified. It was like no sparring I had ever seen or participated in. The students wore headgear with a face cage, chest protector, elbow and knee pads, a groin cup, and MMA training gloves. I'd never seen sparring where you could punch someone straight in the face. It was crazy watching these cats fight. It was like watching a street fight. It was very real and intense. You would see someone getting lit up with punches and then dropped by a spinning back fist, or you would see someone get knocked down by a kick to the head. I even saw some dudes get dropped by groin shots.

The sparring was geared toward fighting in the streets. Sometimes, the fights would end up on the ground, and someone would be slammed or dropped to the floor. But after a few minutes, Sifu would stand the fighters back up to resume sparring. Everyone would fight two rounds. The first round would be hands, feet, elbows, knees, grabbing, and tripping. The second round would be just kicking. Watching these folks spar was intense. I wanted to take a stab at it. I wanted to test myself and see whether I could hang with these guys. So, I ordered my sparring equipment from Sifu. I would keep going to sparring class just as a spectator, taking mental notes. Sometimes I would feel guilty that I was watching and felt that I should be participating, not viewing from the sidelines. The more I watched these guys spar, the more impressed I became. These guys could fight—real ass kickers! I wanted to test myself; I needed it.

So when I finally got my equipment, I decided I would spar in four weeks. My reasoning for this was that I wanted to get used to the equipment, how it felt when I moved. I would go home after class and put on the chest protector and headgear before doing kicks and punches. I had a tough time moving with the chest protector on—I felt like I had no mobility. But I was slowly working my way through it. Wearing the headgear was also tough. I felt claustrophobic, and it was hard to breathe. I decided to first focus on wearing only the headgear while I trained at home. I would shadow-box and jump rope with the headgear on. I wanted to get more comfortable with breathing and seeing while wearing the headgear.

While wearing the headgear, my senses seemed heightened. I could hear my breathing, like it was in 3-D and I was in a video game. It was interesting. For the next month, about twice per week, I would train and jump rope with the headgear on while controlling my breathing and getting comfortable with viewing and hearing with the headgear on. I would even slap myself in the head while wearing it so I could hear, see, and feel what it would be like to get punched or kicked in the face.

The day before I was going to spar, I called up my brother and told him to come over. I needed his help. The doorbell rang, and there was my brother. I put on the headgear and gave him my MMA gloves. He was looking at me in total bewilderment. I told him to just throw punches and slaps my way and all I was going to do was try to block them. I advised him to really try to hit me. He was just standing there in silence and looking at me like I was crazy. He said, "You want me to do what?! Punch you? You're fucking crazy. I'm out of here."

He started to leave. I said, "Wait, look, I'm sparring tomorrow; I just want to get used to the sound and feeling of taking a shot while the headgear is on." It took a lot of convincing on my part, but eventually he agreed. He started throwing punches at me, and all I would do was try to block and parry them. Every now and then, he would tag me with some shots. I remember my brother leaving my apartment, shaking his head, saying, "You're crazy." But I wanted to be prepared. I wanted to hold my own.

I needed to prove something to myself. I was thirty-one, and the last time I had sparred with hard contact was when I was eighteen years old while I was doing Oyama karate, minus the headshots. The sparring these JKD guys did was hardcore. The week I knew I was going to spar, I was nervous.

There was a verse in a song that I couldn't get out of my head that week. It was from an Eminem song and said, "Tear this motherfucking roof off like two dogs caged." I have no idea why, but that was in my head all week and leading up to the day I actually sparred. The day I drove to the school to spar, I remember driving with the radio off, listening to the sound of my tires hitting the road. Doubt and fear starting calling me, teasing me, trying to jump me and beat down my confidence. I started to think, "What if you get knocked out? Or injured?" But then I would counter these negative thoughts with the verse, "Tear this motherfucking roof off like two dogs caged."

It was a constant tug of war of emotions. Thankfully, my mind was too strong to punk out. When I finally got to the school, I parked far away so that no one could see me. The doubt and fear were still trying to attack my mind. I was contemplating leaving. Who would know if I did? Then I started thinking more . . . why do I do this to myself? Just leave. No one will know.

Shakespeare sums up moments like this perfectly when he says, "Boldness, be my friend." There was no way I was going to leave. I was ready for anything. I needed to do this. So, I popped the trunk and grabbed my training bag and sparring equipment. I walked to the door slowly, and when I finally opened it, I knew there was no turning back. I was ready to test myself.

A class was still going on, so I waited in the waiting area. This father who was always there to watch his son training asked me, "So you're going to spar?"

I said yes. He then proceeded to tell me I better hope I didn't spar with some of the senior students because they'd whip my ass. I remember not ever looking at him when I responded, "Good, I'm ready." I just sat in my chair, focusing on my breathing. Trying to maintain a relaxed state. I wore my shin guards on the inside of my sweatpants. I brought my grandparents' mass cards and put them in my shin guards, as I had when I competed in the Taekwondo Junior Olympics. But this time, I had all four of my grandparents' mass cards wrapped in plastic. I put them inside my right shin guard. I just felt the need to have their spirits with me while I sparred. I know it may seem weird to some people, but that's what I did, and it felt natural.

So, I was relaxing in the waiting area. A few people were now in there, including that father who was trying to psych me out. I went into a trance state, something I have done often throughout most of my life. I was just thinking of moves and combos I could do. Stuff I had been working on. Then, I heard the opening of the door that signified that the current class was over, and the sparring class was now open to all eligible students. Only phase two and higher-ranking students could spar.

I walked in, and Sifu greeted me, saying, "Hello, Anthony. Your first sparring class—that's great!"

"Yes, sir," I replied. Then, I felt all the stares of the senior students who were realizing that this was my first sparring class. I walked to the end of the dojo floor where no one was. I took a deep breath and slowly exhaled. I put on the elbow guards, then my sparring cup that I wore on the outside. One senior student came up to me and said, "Are you scared?" I lied and said no. He responded, "Well, you should be." Then, he proceeded to help me put on my chest protector.

I was geared up for battle. I couldn't believe I was actually going through with this. Sifu counted how many students were there so that he could pair us up. He pointed to me and said, "You will spar Fred." I knew Fred from other classes. I'd seen him spar, and he was good. I looked over to Fred and nodded to him as a sign of respect. Fred nodded back. He was about twenty-three and was in better shape than I was.

The first match began. All the students watched as these two guys went at it. What a different experience it was, watching the sparring from the floor. I felt like I was on a street corner, about to watch two gladiators go to war. It was exciting, stressful, and scary all at the same time. Part of me wanted to be next so I could get this over with, and part of me was looking for the exit. It was a matter of time before it would be my turn. I could feel and smell the fear in the air. It was thick and heavy. Then, I heard Sifu call Fred's and my names. I put on my headgear and was comfortable in it; it felt familiar. Conditioning while wearing the headgear prior to going live with sparring had helped.

We squared off, and Sifu had us bow to him and then to each other. I waited about two seconds and then began to bum-rush Fred with kicks and punches. I had a hard time doing high kicks with the chest protector. My kicks came off slow, like I was stuck in the mud. Every time I tried to kick Fred, he would just move out of the way. Kicking just wasn't working for me. So, the majority of strikes came from my punches. I was just attacking Fred, and he was just moving back. I kept throwing punches and landing a lot of clean shots to his head. Sifu told me to watch my power. I could hear other students saying wow.

Fred got in a few good punches and kicks on me. But I felt I had had the better of the exchange. When it was time for the second round, I could see in Fred's eyes that he was tired and frustrated. He too seemed to have respect for my strikes. For both rounds, I held more than my own, though I was more effective in the first round. The second round was just kicks. I was able to get comfortable and find my rhythm. Sifu told me a few times to watch my power. What was crazy was that all the techniques I thought I was going to do while sparring I didn't end up doing. I struggled kicking with the chest protector on: I was slow and telegraphed my kicks. But my punches were connecting. I didn't realize how powerful and fast I was with my hands.

The sparring I had done in the past failed in comparison to this. I could never punch someone in the face while sparring. You could only punch to the body. The only strikes to the head were from kicks. I was happy with myself. I was riding a high wave of confidence. I was so happy that I had faced and completed something that scared me.

As I was leaving the dojo, I went up to Sifu and asked him for feedback. He said I had done well and held my own but that I needed to watch my power. I thanked him for the feedback. Before I left the dojo, I looked back at the empty room with the cold, hard floors and realized I leveled up, today. I conquered my fear. I did something that I was afraid to do, and I did it with bravery and honor. I knew, when I walked out of that dojo, that I was leaving as a new person, a new martial artist. I was leaving better than I'd been when I originally walked in. You can't buy something like that; you can only experience it.

I got in my car and called my brother to tell him the outcome. He was happy for me. I drove home, feeling so proud. I loved the way it felt. Doing something that scares you is a rush. I felt really alive the next day, walking tall and proud. I didn't think I was tough or a badass, but I was proud of myself. The plan was to spar every now and then. That's all I wanted—just enough to test my skills, courage, will, and heart. Looking back, I wish I would have sparred more and learned to be more relaxed, not to go into default mode and brawl. To learn to be calm during the storm and spar with intellect rather than emotion. But this approach is easier said than done. It takes a lot of commitment and guts to reach that level. Nonetheless, I'm still proud of the times I did spar.

My favorite time sparring was against a senior instructor named Rex. This guy was an excellent martial artist, and I had a lot of respect for him. We squared off, bowed to Sifu and then to each other, and began the match. By the time I sparred Rex, I had a few sparring matches under my belt and had learned that the most effective kick for me was the lead hook kick. I would use this kick with the pendulum step to help bridge the gap. From there, I would go right into punches when I was in medium and close range. We were going back and forth, and I was landing some good shots and connecting well with the low lead hook kick. But toward the end of the match, I was feeling gassed, and the tables turned. Rex was landing some wicked strikes and kicks on me. I was glad the round was over. I had started out well, but Rex finished strong. He was a better fighter than I was.

After the first round, Rex told me that he hadn't felt power like that in a long time and that I was a good inside fighter. I thanked him for the compliment while still trying to catch my breath. When it came to the second round, Sifu changed it up. I thought it would be just kicks, but instead it was just hands. As soon as the second round began, Rex lit me up right from jump street. It seemed for every punch I threw, he threw three or four. I was getting winded and overwhelmed. What was even crazier was that Rex was chewing gum while sparring me! His punches were coming in so fast and in bunches. It was very difficult to defend myself from them. It was like driving in a crazy snowstorm when your windshield wipers are unable to keep up and create vision because it's a complete whiteout.

Sifu yelled, "One minute left!" I was completely drained, but I forced myself to finish. What freaked me out was that I noticed at the last minute, Rex eased up on the punches, putting much less power into them. He knew I was toast and felt bad for me. I couldn't believe this guy was giving me a pass. I had been throwing heat at this dude, strong punches and kicks, and he still took it easy on me. I couldn't understand that. If someone was hitting me as hard as I was hitting him and was getting tired and winded, I would have taken advantage of that moment.

After class, I asked Rex why he'd taken it easy on me. He just looked at me and said, "I'm supposed to do that—you're still learning." I replied, "Sir, I don't know if I could have done what you did tonight." Rex looked me right in the eyes and said, "You would have done the same thing." Still confused and humbled, I shook his hand and thanked him for the lesson. Rex was a real martial artist that had no ego. A rare breed. I know for a fact that most students, including senior students, would not have held back. Rex's actions, attitude, and approach inspired me. It was the best ass-whipping I ever got. That's something I love about martial arts: you are always growing and learning. You build, break, and build again.

It never ends; there is always a lesson to be learned. Every action has a cause and effect. That sparring match changed me as a martial artist for the better. It made me see things on a deeper level. Sparring can be a trick bag. Over the years, studying many types of martial arts, I have seen many good martial artists quit because they had bad experiences in sparring. What a tragedy. I have found that sparring can be the graveyard of shattered dreams for some martial artists, especially new ones. Again, this is just my opinion, and I'm certainly no authority. When it's your first time sparring, I think it's prudent to be prepared for it. The first thing I would do is watch a few sparring classes. See how it goes down. Analyze the fighters and their techniques. Take it all in. Then start to build on your game.

Start jumping rope to build up your wind. See whether you can do pre-sparring practice so you can prepare before you go live. Wear your equipment and have a training partner throw punches at you with not much power while you just block. This serves two purposes: you work on your blocks and parries, and you slowly condition your body and mind to get hit. I think many martial artists panic the first time they spar because they are overwhelmed by the fear and anxiety of getting hit. That's why I had my brother slap and punch me, not too hard, when I had my headgear on before I went live with sparring. It gave me an advantage on how not to panic when I got tagged in the head. I didn't enjoy getting hit, but I was able to handle it better.

Also, during pre-sparring, you can work on throwing punches and kicks with a training partner in a controlled, relaxing setting. Always remember partner preservation when training with other people. Some martial artists forget about this. Respect your training partner. End and begin with respect. Another important thing to remember when sparring is not to be outcome dependent and think you must come out the winner and dominate your opponent. Instead, focus on the act of sparring, on showing courage and bravery that you're doing something that scares you. You're going to step up and face your fear. That's living!

Keep in mind that if you spar with someone and get outclassed, outpowered, or outworked, you still faced your opponent with heart and bravery. You already won. That ain't no bullshit, either! You leveled up and grew stronger as a person and martial artist. Think about it: you're playing in traffic and taking risks. Putting your ego and pride on the chopping block. That is honorable. Most people go through life just talking shit from the sidelines, never taking any risks, just playing it safe. Some of them will even have the strongest opinions on your performance, all from the safety of the sidelines. Just give them the "fuck you" smile and use their toxic energy as motivation for your journey. I kind of pity some of these people because they don't realize they are wasting their lives. Not having the courage or belief in themselves to take chances to improve. The real tragedy is when they wake up one day with the "Would have, could have, and should have" feeling of regret.

I think one of the most beautiful sights in the martial arts world is when someone is getting lit up in sparring and outclassed as a martial artist but won't give up. The person keeps moving forward, being relentless, and feeling an overload of fear, exhaustion, and shame. The person keeps at it, stalking the opponent, taking punishment from all the strikes and kicks. It's remarkable and inspirational to see someone with that type of will.

For instance, I was once watching two teenagers sparring. One kid was an experienced, gifted, cocky martial artist, and the other was a kid I had never seen before. The experienced student was working this new kid good, hitting him with shots and kicks with ease and power. Just beating the hell out of him. But the kid who was getting punished just kept coming for this star of the dojo, moving forward. He had this look in his eyes that said he wanted to destroy this kid, regardless of the fact that he was getting the shit kicked out of him. This kid had no fear, and his will was strong. I could see and feel his focused gaze through his headgear. The kid refused to give into the pain he was feeling from all the shots he was taking. He just kept pushing on, trying to land his own strikes, and he did a few times. It appeared this kid had hardly any training in fighting. It was heart and balls with him. Someone who had no martial arts experience would watch that fight and say that the senior student kicked that kid's ass all over the floor, that the kid had no business sparring. But someone who has trained in the martial arts for a long time would recognize the warrior heart that the kid possessed. He had no quitting in him and controlled his fear.

If that had been a street fight, that kid might have had a good chance of beating the skillful martial artist kid. One kid was fighting to show off his skills, and the other guy was fighting to survive with a stronger spirit. After the sparring class, the new kid looked dejected; he hung is head low in shame. It killed me to see him like that. I went up to him and introduced myself. He said his name was Dion. I told him that he'd done a great job and that he had a strong warrior spirit. He seemed to think I was mocking him. I told him I was serious and asked him how long he'd been training in the martial arts. He said he had no prior training and that this was the first time he'd ever sparred. I laughed out loud.

I said, "Dude, you just sparred a very skillful martial artist and held your own. The kid you fought was a top-tier student, and you ate all his punches and kicks. You did great. You should be proud of yourself. But you must keep training!" Dion thanked me for telling him that. He thought he'd done terribly. He needed to hear that he'd done well, and I'm glad I'm the one who told him. Now, that match could be a reference point for him for the rest of his training and in his life. He could know that he had it in him to do amazing things.

But the real joy was watching this kid continue to train and grow as a martial artist. As time went by, Dion's ability and skill as a martial artist became equal to his heart and warrior spirit. When you have skill and heart as a martial artist, you are dangerous to any opponent. Every now and then, I think of the impact I had on Dion. The look in his eyes was pitiful before I gave him a pep talk, and it makes me feel good that I reset his perception of that experience and empowered him to continue to train in the martial arts. The more I think about it, I was just returning the favor because when I was about eighteen years old, some dude reached out to me after a tough sparring match when I felt defeated and thought I sucked as a martial artist. Lee told me I'd done great in my sparring match and that I was a natural. That kept me training. Who knows—maybe one day Dion will do the same thing for some kid he sees not having a good day sparring. Karma can be beautiful.

Time was flying while I was training in JKD. After two years in phase two, I was selected to test for phase three. I couldn't believe it. I was in shock and didn't see that coming. And to be honest, I was in no rush to advance; I just wanted to learn and make techniques my own. My motto was, "When it's time, it's time." I wasn't going to rush it or force it.

Other students would ask when they would be tested for the next phase all the time. I never asked. I wanted to earn it based on my performance, let it flow to me. Don't get me wrong—the idea of advancing in my martial arts training was a goal and accomplishment for me. Putting in hard work and dedication in training and being recognized by your teacher and rewarded a new rank is truly a feeling of supreme achievement. That being said, a higher rank or belt does not necessarily mean you're a better martial artist than the guy below you. It's more of an individual conquest while you're on your journey. You're always in competition with yourself. Participating and watching JKD sparring and seeing how it humbles students, as when a lower-ranking student outworks a senior rank student, is always interesting. It doesn't happen often, but when it does, it makes me realize how nothing is certain and to never underestimate an opponent.

Phase three classes were private, and the curtains were pulled down. Sifu was teaching some high-level stuff, and he wanted to keep it closed to the public. Phase three was on another level. I was learning so much so fast—how to think and act like a martial artist twenty-four seven. I learned a lot in phase three; it seemed like there was always something else to discover. I was introduced to weapons such as the knife and single stick. The more I was learning, the more I realized I needed to keep training. Many times, I was nervous to go to class because the intensity level was always high, and the senior students took training very seriously.

I would also get frustrated with myself. I was learning high-level stuff that was highly involved and required level skill to comprehend and apply. Sometimes, training was tough, and I would leave bummed out. I couldn't understand the technique and felt that I was annoying my training partners because I was holding them back. Most martial artists can relate to this, and it is something you need to understand and accept. Develop patience and gratitude. I learned to embrace the frustration, roam out of my comfort zone, and just be patient and practice.

It's also important to ask for help and feedback. Everybody gets scared and nervous to some degree while training in martial arts—whether it's getting hurt, being afraid, not knowing the correct answer and being wrong, or being embarrassed by someone. As I've said before, we are our own worst critics sometimes. We need to realize that mistakes will be made and that things won't always go the way we want. But what is important is how we respond to these challenges and move on and grow from them, not letting them nest in our heads and poison our minds. Kick it the fuck out of your mind. Don't take yourself so seriously; have fun and laugh at yourself.

When I got frustrated with my training, I would reflect on how far I had come and how much I had accomplished. I was fulfilling my dream as an aspiring martial artist. I remind myself of the martial artist I was before I learned JKD—as different as night and day. The insight and techniques I learned have truly changed my life for the better.

I was living the dream—I was training three times per week, had a great job, and was making money. I was working a job that I had progressed in, moving up the corporate ranks all on my own thanks to my work ethic and commitment to excellence. I was also proud that through my hard work and persistence, I became a good bartender. Things were cool for me on so many levels, but martial arts were my core. My anchor. My balance. It gave me the confidence to pursue the things I wanted and the strength and mental endurance to handle and overcome any setback. After all, you will never know when you will have to use your martial arts. It's not likely you will get an e-mail reminder that today you'll be attacked, so you must train and be ready for anything. Practice with persistent passion and then repeat. Most important, learn to react quickly and with confidence to a possible attacker or sucker punch that life throws at you.

Chapter 9: Six Months' Severance: Climbing the ladder again

"Life is not about how fast you run or how high you climb but how well you bounce."
—Vivian Komori

In 2009, I was let go from my job that I'd gotten right out of college. I had been there for ten years, and I achieved a lot while working there, including being promoted five times. I was making good money, and for five out of the ten years, I had a company car. What I achieved was all from hard work and a strong will. There were some tough times while I was working there. I was sometimes overwhelmed with work from a new position and had to supervise difficult people, but I always stuck it out and made it work.

But like always, the confidence and bravery that I obtained from training in martial arts overflowed into my work life. In June 2009, my entire department was let go. It was tough for many people all over the country: many hardworking people lost their jobs. The last day I drove to the office I was filled with sadness, shock, anger, and fear about what to do next. After ten years, I was given a six-month severance package. The VP wished me well and shook my hand. It was tough saying goodbye to some of my co-workers. We all promised to keep in touch with one another, and a lot of people were breaking down, overwhelmed by the sadness. I stayed strong.

While driving home from the office, I started to get this overwhelming feeling. I was light-headed and felt nervous. I pulled over at a rest stop that overlooked the Hudson River. I realized I must have been having a panic attack. I turned the car off and got out. While looking at the river, I was trying to control my breathing. I started to calm down and tried to get back to a relaxed state. I just stood there, gazing at the river, realizing that I was furious I'd been let go from my job. I wondered what I'd do for money. Then, I just focused on my blind faith and told myself that I would be OK. I got back in the car and drove to my favorite Italian deli. I ordered a big hero sandwich, a bag of chips, and a soda. I ate it and took a long nap. When I awoke, I was still angry but decided not to dwell on it too long.

The next day, which was Saturday, I was scheduled to bartend, and I was glad. I wanted to keep myself busy. I was working with my good friend and mentor, Turk. He knew what was going on, and we talked all the time. During the shift, I would go quiet and just think about what had happened. Then, all of a sudden, while I was in my trance, Turk threw a bar towel at me to get my attention. I looked at him with confusion. He looked right at me and said, "You got this. You got this. Now you're going to see what you're made of. My money is on you, kid."

Those words struck a chord in my soul, reminding me who I was—a ninja, samurai, and Spartan all in one. That I could accomplish anything I put my mind to. I thanked Turk for the talk. He was the type of dude you could call at 4 a.m. if you were in a jam.

The next day, I came up with a game plan. I was going to take off July and August. The only thing I was going to do was train at JKD three times per week and train at home. I would look for jobs in late August. That July and August were all about training and reading martial arts books. I was in peak mode. I shifted all my focus to training and working on my craft. Reading my old training journals from the summer of 2009, I can tell I was on point. I would wake up and jump rope for seven minutes straight with no skips, shadow-box for fifteen minutes, and end with one hundred push-ups in sets of twenty. I did not dwell on the fact that I no longer had a job and would have to find one after being out of the market for ten years. Again, I just went by my blind belief.

This faith in myself has given me an edge in life. The ultimate goal for a martial artist is total connection among body, mind, and spirit. I have always been able to formulate a solid game plan and stay motivated when it comes to important moments in my life, plotting and planning while maintaining a positive attitude. My mentality is unbreakable. My martial arts training made me realize that everything I need is within me. With a strong mind, body, heart, and focus, I can draw from within myself the strength to accomplish anything—to walk alone and be alone, if necessary. It takes real strength to stand alone during difficult times in your life. My blind belief and training have been my sword and shield to protect me from life's cruelties and setbacks.

Toward the end of August, I started my job search. The first job I applied to was for a telecommunication company as a retention specialist. What this entailed was if someone called to cancel cell phone service, it was my job to save the account and prevent the customer from canceling. This was an entry-level job, and the salary they were offering was less than half of what I was making at my prior job. I had a plan. I wanted to work while I was still getting the rest of my severance pay so that I could save as much money as possible. I also wanted to try something in a totally different field. When I was doing my research on this company, I found that the turnover rate for this job was very high, and the employee comments online were horrible. I didn't care—I kind of knew this gig was not going to be permanent. My main goal was to save money. I also had a white-belt mentality: I wanted to learn new skills and add them to my arsenal.

When I went in for an interview, the first thing I had to do was take a test. I was a little taken aback by that. The test was nothing too crazy, though. I waited for my results. If you did well on the test, you were asked to come back for another interview, and I was. At the second interview, I was hitting it off very well with the interviewer. I vocalized that I was trained very well in customer service at my prior job and had met and exceeded goals. The woman who was interviewing me was impressed but had some concerns. She stated, "I think you are overqualified for this position, and your prior salary (I had to disclose my salary on the application) is nowhere near what we are offering you." Then she said, "I don't even think you're going to like your job."

I explained that I was aware of her concerns but wanted to possibly change my career path and knew that would mean a pay cut. I reminded her that I had just been let go after being somewhere for ten years and so was trying to reinvent myself. After an hour of talking, she offered me the job and told me I would start in September 2009—just as I'd planned. Train like a warrior in July and August and start a new job in September. It made me feel confident in trusting my blind faith.

My first day at the job was interesting, to say the least. A lot of people were starting at the same time as I was, and after talking with them, I came to realize that most of them were in the same predicament—just laid off. We all wanted to find our rhythm and get back to where we were before we got axed from our jobs. It was unspoken, but we all could tell it. Working at this place I knew had a short shelf life, by my own choice. After four months, I would start looking for a new job. But I did learn some cool things and meet some great people from all walks of life while working there. But this was the first time, and hopefully the last time, I would ever work at a call center.

The management would treat their people like garbage. Somebody would quit or get fired about every other day. The first six weeks of working at this telecommunication call center, I was with a group of twenty new hires for training from nine to six. I still was able to train at JKD twice per week. After the training period was over, my new hours were 1 to 10 p.m. My JKD training almost came to a complete stop. The only time I could train was when I had a day off during the week. I went from going twice or three times per week to twice per month. But I had to make do.

I was still doing my bartending hustle. I used tips to buy the BOB punching bag, which is short for body opponent bag. This free-standing punching bag helped me with my solo training. I did not want to lose my skills and edge. Every morning before work, around 10 a.m., I would jump rope for ten minutes straight. It took a year, but I worked and built my stamina back up, which was another proud moment of accomplishing a goal I set for myself. I would do this every morning for five days of the week. It would shock my body, and I was out of breath every time I finished. I really pushed through the pain, developing a strong mind, focus, and mental endurance. Then, when I came home after work, I would work out on the BOB bag, do some shadow-boxing, and do push-ups. It was painful that I could not train for JKD like I wanted, and I feared losing the skills that had taken me a long time to develop.

Training at home kept me focused and committed to my craft. The times I was able to train at the JKD school, people would comment that they hadn't seen me for a while but then would tell me that they could see I had been training at home by the way I was performing in class. That made me feel good and eased my mind. The thing you have to remember in martial arts is that skills are hard to come by, and they take years and many hours to develop. If you don't give them the attention, effort, and respect they deserve, you will lose them.

I lasted five months at that call center. In February 2010, I landed an interview with a big auto collection center. The position was for a collection supervisor. This interview I was going on was a difficult one that included a panel with three people in the room and two other people on the phone. The purpose of the interview was for each interviewer to be able to ask a question, and after I was done answering, they would grade it. After the interview was complete, the interviewers would compare notes and give me a final grade before deciding whether I'd passed and qualified for the position.

I felt very confident about obtaining the job. Based on my ten years of experience and all the different positions I held while I was at my previous job, I was prepared for these types of interviews. These were the types of interviews you had to complete to advance to your next career goal. In fact, my prior company trained its employees to answer questions in interviews in a specific format so that all areas were covered while they answered the questions. It was a very effective approach, and I customized it to fit my style. I called it SPAR (situation problem action result). This is how it works. During the interview, you're asked, "Describe a time you had to deal with a difficult customer who was not happy. What did you do to resolve that customer's needs? What was the outcome?" You would give the situation, then the problem it caused, then the action you took, and then the final result. I looked at this SPAR concept as a punching combo; it just clicked for me. I was able to make it flow and give solid, passionate answers.

The panel interview was a week away, and I practiced every night. I had no idea what they were going to ask me. So, what I did was go online and research common questions asked during an interview. I would just drill this every night and apply my SPAR technique. The more I practiced, the more confident and comfortable I became. I would practice in my apartment, talking to the walls. Sounds crazy, I know, but it's very competitive out there, and I wanted to always be on point.

The big day finally came. There I was in the conference room with three managers and two other managers on the phone. One of the managers in the room looked at me and said, "Are you ready to begin?" I looked at him with a smile and said, "Yes, sir." I was ready for this. I was ready to hold my own. Each manager would ask a question, and I would pause, then answer, using my SPAR technique. As I was talking, they would write things down. I was not fazed by what they wrote. I just focused on answering the questions in the best way I could, all ground covered. It was me versus five corporate soldiers. A few of them tried to trip me up with questions and responses to my answers. But I held my own: I was crushing it.

The interview lasted about ninety minutes. After I was done, I thanked everyone in the room and on the phone for their time and the opportunity. They advised me that human resources would contact me in a few days with the final result. I left feeling very confident that I had scored this gig. I remember driving home very proud based on the fact that these guys were firing all these questions at me, and I was giving solid answers. As always, I just relied on my blind belief, instinct, and confidence.

Three days later, I got a call from the HR department, telling me the folks who interviewed me were impressed, and that the job was mine. I showed up to the call center the next day, feeling quite happy. I had lasted five months at this place and saved a lot of my severance pay—two goals that I set for myself. I was so relieved to leave that place, but I had humbled myself by sticking it out.

The call center served its purpose for me. It was a great feeling to walk out for the last time.

I was excited to start my next gig. I was making more money and slowly climbing back up to my previous salary. This place was far from my house, over an hour both ways. My first day at the collection center was a little weird. I met the director, Larry. He was in charge of fifty employees and the overall operations of the collection center. I went to his office, and he wanted to get to know me. He hadn't been there for my panel interview. However, he advised me that he was impressed with the feedback he received regarding my interview. He began to tell me about himself. He had this big sign in his office that said, "The Boss," and as he kept talking, I realized how full of himself this guy was. He was so over the top. But I just sat there and listened.

Larry then said, "Do you know why I have this sign my office?" I said, "Because you're the boss?" He said, "Bingo! This place is my ship, my candy store, and I run it like a tight operation. I see and hear everything. Just look at the awards on my wall for top performer." I looked at Larry and said, "Very impressive."

I was having such mixed feelings at this point. Then Larry informed me that he wanted to take me to lunch with three other managers. He closed the meeting by telling me what he expected from me and that I would be supervising ten people who needed to be coached and developed. I responded, "Understood," and I meant it. That was the only part of our meeting that I liked. Tell me what you want, and I will take it from there.

Boss Larry walked around the business center and introduced me to all the people. He was walking around with an unlit cigar in his mouth. The people seemed to be afraid of Larry, and he seemed to enjoy and feed off their fear. He then introduced me to the people I would be supervising. They looked like a tough group; they seemed broken and bitter. I knew right then and there, between Boss Larry and this crew, that I would have a full plate. I went up to each one of them, all ten, and introduced myself, and I asked each of them for their name. Most of them gave me a quick, fake smile and quickly went back to their desks.

I was so dizzy at this point, overwhelmed. Boss Larry and three other managers took me out for lunch. I did this under silent protest. I didn't want to go. While at lunch, Boss Larry held court, and everything he said, the three managers would agree with. If Larry made a failed attempt at humor, all three managers would laugh. I was getting sick to my stomach. I never was and never will be a suck-up. I work hard, and I respect everyone, but I'm not a phony, especially not someone who kisses ass, thinking it will advance his career. I would force a smile and laugh just to blend in and seem like a team player. After all, this was my first day.

I think Boss Larry was taken aback by my confidence and how I spoke quite frankly. I think he was intimidated. I wasn't feeling this place or the people at all. It had bad vibes. I wasn't used to this type of paper tiger mentality in management. How I missed my old job. I was blessed to have been there for ten years and to be groomed and developed by true leaders who led by example and empowered their employees. This place was the complete opposite. I noticed that everybody was a yes man, and everyone seemed to be afraid to make a decision on their own, especially the managers. They would run everything by Boss Larry first. This type of behavior was frowned upon at my old job. It shows you have no confidence in your abilities. How can you lead people if you can't lead yourself? I was starting to panic, but I calmed myself down and made a mental promise to myself: give it three months and then re-evaluate the situation.

My hours were 9am to 5pm with one late night per week. I would have to leave at 7:10 a.m. to get to work by 9 a.m. If I left later, I would hit traffic and arrive late. What made matters even worse was that my JKD school was two hours from my new job. It was hard to make class, and if I did make it, I was shot. I would be drained mentally from the commute and not being happy at work. Things were not going according to plan, and my training suffered. After three months, I re-evaluated the job, and it got worse. Boss Larry and the management team would talk a good game on how to run and maintain a winning team. But when it came to disciplining employees or dealing with a difficult situation, they would all fold like a cheap suit, and Boss Larry was the biggest offender. All bark, no bite. All show, no go. This place would have these huddles throughout the work day, and everybody would just agree with whatever Boss Larry said.

I wanted to slap some of these guys. Like how Don Corleone slaps Johnny Fontane in *The Godfather* and says, "You can act like a man." This place was bizarre. There were a few times I spoke up and tried to offer some insight or suggestions. Boss Larry would always shoot me down and say he wasn't sure about my idea, and then the entire management team would just agree with him and collectively reject whatever idea I presented. Many times, I was so dejected and mentally drained from work that I had no desire to train. In my experience, when you have a lot on your mind and are not in a good place, training can be dangerous. You have to be focused at all times. If you're lost in space, you can end up hurting yourself or your training partner because your focus is polluted by your negative mental chatter. I had to get out and leave this job ASAP. Thank God for my family, who always offered me encouragement and allowed me to call them on my way home from work and vent. My family has always been a powerful source of strength and support from day one.

Sometimes I would force myself to go to training, and afterward, I was glad I went because I would leave in a better state of mind. That training made me happy, and the more I thought about it, I had to make do with what I had to work with. Some training is better than no training. After I accepted that, I felt better. I also had a catharsis, a breakthrough: I needed to leave my old job in the past. I needed to stop comparing it to my current job and future jobs. The only way for me to move forward was to leave that job in the past. I was very lucky to have that experience. But I could no longer be a prisoner of my past. I had to constantly remind myself that emptying your cup applied to all aspects of your life.

So after seven months at this job, I was ready to move on. I received a phone call from a former co-worker, who advised me that there was a position available where he worked. It was the same industry: auto loans and collections. This job was a lot closer to my house and offered more money. I told my friend I was interested, and he told me who I had to call to set up an interview. I made that phone call quickly and set up the interview. The interview was quick; my friend was doing well there and vouched for me. The next day, I received an e-mail with a job offer. That quick and I had a new job. All I could think of was that this was my third job within a year after being at one place for ten years. I was also surprised that my salary was almost back to where it was when I got laid off. I thought about how tough the previous year had been for me and all the drama, stress, frustration, and anger I went through. But I realized it had made me stronger and that I had held my own during an unforeseen career change.

The next day, I went to Larry's office. He looked at me, and I said, "Boss, I need to talk with you." It was the first time I had ever addressed him as "Boss." It just came out. I told him that I had a better job offer and that I was moving on from his candy store. He just looked at me and didn't say anything, like he couldn't care less. But I knew it bothered him. I wasn't a big fan of Larry, mainly because of his leadership skills, but I was respectful toward him, even at the end. Believe me, I wanted to vocalize my dissatisfaction about the overall management style of the center. Larry had a false confidence, and I felt he was doing a disservice to his employees. Respect is earned, not given or bought. Nevertheless, I thanked Larry for the opportunity, and I rode off into the sunset. I left that place and never looked back. I was ready for my new gig. No more comparing jobs. I wanted a career with stability.

Starting this new job, I was so focused on making it work. It's my third job in the last year is what I kept telling myself over and over. This gig was intense, and everyone worked really hard. The company paid well and expected a lot out of every employee. It was a fast-paced environment, and you had to pick up quickly on everything that was going on. I was overwhelmed many times and left work feeling lousy and mad at myself for not picking up things more quickly, but I kept at it and kept reminding myself that I could do anything I wanted when I put my mind and effort toward achieving my chosen goal. I would make a list of obstacles I accomplished in my life such as winning a silver medal, graduating college, and overcoming all of my roadblocks. How I stuck to my promise and stayed on my martial arts journey. I would do this over and over to the point that, when I felt myself getting overwhelmed from my job, my mind would automatically think of the great things I had achieved. I would see these achieved goals in my mind. I would counter my negative mindset with a positive one. It was crazy. This job was in my mental GPS, and I was going to get to my destination, come hell or high water. Every time I found myself comparing my new job to my old one, I would mentally see and hear STOP and say to myself, "Empty your cup." I was hell-bent on making this job work.

The first two months were brutal, and I had to learn by trial and error. If I made a mistake, it would sting for weeks. I just kept at it, kept going, kept moving forward. Some of the people weren't the nicest to me. I was the new guy, back to being a white belt. I was humbled. I took whatever shit they gave me. I just stayed focused on my target to become great at my new job. By the third month, things got a little better, and I was getting more comfortable and confident with what I was doing. It wasn't easy, but I kept my head down and did my work with an intense focus. As time went by, I felt less stress from the job, and that was a good feeling. I wanted to get back to training ASAP. In the previous year, my martial arts focus had suffered greatly, and I was committed to amplifying myself as a martial artist—not to just training at my JKD school but to changing it up a bit.

Chapter 10: Hitting Mitts

"You can't wait for inspiration.
You have to go after it with a club."
—Jack London

There was a boxing gym close to where I worked. One day, I went in and inquired about taking private lessons, doing some mitt work. This was something I had always wanted to do to get an edge with my striking, so the plan was that I would take lessons just working on my hands. I set up a lesson with one of the instructors for right after work. His name was Coach Mike. Mike was a former boxer who was now a trainer. My first impression was that he was a no-nonsense type of guy. Mike asked whether I had had any boxing training. I said no but that I had been training in jeet kune do for the last five years and that I was a right-handed fighter who liked to fight with my power side forward. Coach Mike just looked at me with massive confusion, shaking his head.

He said, "You're a righty, but you fight like a southey?" I said, "What's a southey?" He said it was short for southpaw. He still had a confused look on his face as to why I would want to do that. But then he said, "Whatever. Let's do this." I put on my gloves. Coach Mike asked me, "What about your wraps?" I said I didn't have any and had never used them before. He just looked at me again and said,

"Oh, boy!" He began to laugh. He then asked me whether I was ready. I said, "Yes, sir."

He started feeding me the mitts and yelled for me to do a jab. I threw a jab, which gave a loud pop. Mike called out "double jab," and I threw two quick, powerful jabs. He looked at me and said, "OK, nice power." As if he were surprised I had some skill. Then he told me what punches to throw: jab, cross, jab, cross, and hook. Most of the time when I was hitting the mitts, I would hear a loud pop. Some people were staring at me while I was striking. I can't lie: I was digging the attention. In between the punches, Coach Mike pointed out things I needed to fix and taught me some new concepts such as head placement, foot placement, and single-hand combinations. The lesson lasted over thirty minutes. I was working hard the entire time. I had a one-minute rest between each round.

I think Coach Mike was impressed with my footwork, cardio, and power. From my first lesson hitting mitts, I was hooked. The rush I got from hitting those mitts was amazing. I felt creative, like I was playing an instrument. The sound I was creating every time I hit the mitts was like music. A loud pop and slap echoed throughout the gym. I felt the people staring at me. I was moving smoothly. Plus, it was a great workout and total creative outlet for me. I was in my own world. I was so pumped up after my first session that I quickly scheduled another one with Coach Mike. My goal was to do mitt work to help improve my striking and make me a better martial artist.

This new training gave me the spark that I needed. It got me excited again and put me back on course for my martial arts journey. For the past year, I had just been going through the motions with my training. I think it kept me sane while dealing with all the new job drama I was going through. I took a lesson with Coach Mike once per week. After each lesson, he would offer insight into what I had done well and what I needed to work on. Coach Mike kept it real and never sugarcoated anything when it came to our training sessions. I was also back to training at the JKD school twice per week. I was growing as a martial artist. That was my goal. I felt good, and my striking was improving.

I trained weekly with Coach Mike for about six months. Then it came to a complete stop. He was training boxers for the Golden Gloves, so all his focus and time were dedicated to those guys. I was able to get a lesson in once per month. I had to take what I could get, and I was extremely thankful for all the lessons I had with him. Some of my JKD training partners noticed the improvements in my striking and would tell me. It felt good to hear it, especially after all the hard work and time I was putting in. I didn't tell many people I was cross-training, only a few. I kept it to myself. It was my business and my journey. I started to notice a reoccurring conclusion when I was training and learning new things: the more I learned, the less I realized I knew. "Technique" was the word that entered my mind all the time on my martial arts journey. It never ends; training and learning never end.

It was 2011. Things were progressing at my new job. I had made it one year, and things were going well there. I was slowly finding my groove and building my career back up brick by brick. I was still training at JKD, but I missed doing mitts with Coach Mike, so I started looking for other striking coaches. I came across this boxer, Russ. My first lesson with Coach Russ was on a Saturday. I scheduled it for 6 p.m. I met Russ in the gym parking lot. The gym was closed, but he had the key code to get in. The gym had twenty-four-hour access. We were the only ones in the gym. Russ started me out with jump rope. I did three two-minute rounds. Coach Russ was familiar with my background because we'd talked on the phone prior to our meeting up. I advised him that I was interested in improving my striking skills. I told him that I was really interested in doing mitts and training with him, silently thinking that I could pick up where I left off with Coach Mike. But I quickly realized that Russ's style of hitting mitts was much different from Mike's style. Coach Russ wanted to work on the fundamentals of boxing. This guy lived, slept, and ate boxing. He was a wealth of information.

He would have me do footwork drills and then have me step and jab from one end of the gym and back.

Besides being a great boxer, Russ was a good teacher. He took his time explaining technique and theory. The way he broke things down was brilliant. He would explain his theory on sparring—that it takes one hundred rounds of sparring just to get truly comfortable with it. That if you're getting hit while sparring, you shouldn't get mad at the guy tagging you; instead, get mad at yourself. It's your fault you're getting hit, not his. Then Coach Russ would end things by saying, "Think about it."

He was constantly dropping gems of knowledge on me. He would say that boxing is based on deception. Like in doing magic tricks, work on your tricks. He would emphasize how important it is to practice in front of the mirror, watch yourself, and pick up on your bad habits and correct them. Coach Russ brilliantly explained his approach to shadow-boxing and what it meant to him. He approached shadow-boxing as if he had just gotten sucker-punched and was reacting and recovering at the same time.

He also taught me a cool move to practice: stay in one place, keep your hands up to protect your face, and practice pivoting on your front foot and back foot. This was a great way to build up your punching power by learning to pivot on your punches. He said his boxing coach and mentor swore by this and would practice it for hours, that it served so many purposes: developing a tight guard, body awareness for pivoting, and tremendous punching power. Every time I trained with Coach

Russ, we would go over an hour, sometimes two, but he always charged me for one hour.

I had about ten lessons with Coach Russ in the span of four months. He would also occasionally send motivational—sometimes annoying—texts to all his boxing students on the weekends. The text would go out at 9 a.m. and would read: "Just finished a two mile run and did twelve rounds of shadow-boxing. Let me guess, you're probably still sleeping?" It would annoy and motivate me at the same time. I began to realize that my martial arts journey was taking me in a new direction, into the entry level of boxing. I was excited. I was meeting cool people and learning new things to improve my game. I was on this new path, and I just wanted to keep trying different trainers to improve my game. It was an expensive quest! I tried many trainers, and some of them just didn't click with me. Coach Mike and Coach Russ were the best, and they had set the bar high.

I was still training at JKD, trying to make it to two classes per week when I could. Even though where I worked was closer to the dojo than my last job had been, the commute was still far and at times draining. But I still kept going when I could, and most of the time, I walked out better. Regardless of whether I was motivated or frustrated, I was growing as a martial artist. I was still doing my solo training at home, doing a lot of mirror work, and watching how I punched, held my hands, blocked, and parried. It was 2012, and I had been at my new job for two years; I was so happy and relieved. I was doing very well, making a name for myself. Then all of sudden, out of nowhere, while I was at my JKD class, Sifu handed me a certificate letting me know that I had advanced to another phase of training. I couldn't believe it. The last time I had been promoted was in 2008. I was extremely grateful and began to self-reflect: this was another proud accomplishment on my martial arts journey. Even while I'm writing this, I am so proud of myself and thankful that I found this JKD school, met Sifu, and had the discipline, courage, and dedication to stick it out. I was in a good place. I realized that I could handle the tough winds and waves life sends me.

I decided I wanted to step it up with my cross-training, so I planned a trip to Vegas to go to a well-known MMA gym, take private lessons, and improve my striking and kicking. I had always wanted to go to Vegas and train in the fight Mecca of the world. So, I booked my trip and lessons three months in advance. I was still bartending, so the money I made between tips and the shift pay would help pay for the trip and lessons. I know I keep bringing up bartending throughout this book, but it has been a big part of my journey too. My martial arts training provided me with the mental edge and thick skin to deal with the early pressures of tending bar. The ups and downs I went through. Martial arts gave me the mindset to fall, stand, and repeat. Sometimes when I bartend, I'm reminded of how I destroyed and overcame this tough obstacle, how hard it was for me, and how I now use bartending as a side hustle.

Chapter 11: Going to Vegas: The Martial Arts Hobbyist and the Real Fighters

"Do not try to fight a lion if you are **not** one yourself."
—African Proverb

So, the day finally arrived for my trip to Vegas. In the plane, I imagined how the training would go down. What would the place look like? After getting there, I would wake up early before I went to my training sessions. I went to the hotel gym and ran on the treadmill for thirty minutes. I was getting anxious. I went back to my room, got ready, grabbed my gear, and prayed that I would make the most out of this experience. Then I got in a cab, and off I went. Before I entered the gym, I just stayed outside, taking it all in and mentally preparing.

I went in and introduced myself to the nice lady at the front desk. I'd arrived there early; I had twenty minutes to kill. She told me I could sit in the waiting area and watch the class. I started to bug out. This place was really big. It had matted floors and a big boxing ring. There were all kinds of cool MMA and boxing pictures on the walls. I was just about to take private lessons at one of the best MMA gyms in Vegas and possibly the world. I was watching all that was going on. Everyone who was training, both men and women, was in fantastic shape. Everyone seemed to have a gallon of water, and in between the workouts, some of them would eat a can of tuna, banana, or low-fat yogurt.

These men and women were real fighters. They all had the same look in their eyes: a deep, focused, thousand-yard stare. And the closer I got, I could see the battle scars on their faces and their noses and ears deformed from all the rigorous training and fights they had seen in the cage or ring. I'll keep it real with you: I was very imitated at this point. But I knew I needed and wanted this experience. It was going to change me. Then I met the first instructor for my first training session. His name was Steve. Coach Steve was the head boxing coach.

My first meeting with Steve was good. He was nice and asked about my martial arts background and what I was looking to gain and learn. However, once I started to train with Coach Steve, his attitude changed: he became very negative and short with me. It almost seemed like he was annoyed to even be training with me. But it didn't faze me one bit. I wasn't looking or expecting any pats on the back. I wanted to learn and improve, and I was ready for whatever this dude would throw at me. For the first fifteen minutes, Steve ripped apart how I punched and everything else I did. I just listened and took everything he dished at me. I showed no anger or frustration toward his comments. After all, I was there to learn and walk out better than I'd come in. I took it as a challenge not to let this dude break me.

The more negative he was toward me, the more respect I showed him. I think I impressed Coach Steve with my mental endurance. He started to be a little nicer to me. I think he was feeling me out and realized I did not have a big ego, bad attitude, or delusions that I was the next big thing. He started to let his guard down and began to show me some skills. I was so focused. Ready to learn. Ready for this mission.

Coach Steve brought me into the ring, and we began to do some mitt work. He had his own way of doing it. Steve told me that I fought too close and needed to back up after I struck. Coach Steve had to tell me this a few times. Then he would throw some punches at me to see how I defended. He was throwing quick punches at me, but I was blocking and parrying most of his strikes.

While we were training in the ring, a young fighter in his early twenties came in the ring in a frantic manner and said, "Coach Steve, I cut my face." He had a small but deep gash on his right cheek. Coach Steve examined the cut for a few seconds, then told the kid he was OK and to go in the bathroom to clean it off and put Krazy Glue on it. Krazy Glue! The kid kept saying, "But I got cut, and it was clear he was not happy with Coach Steve's response or lack of concern regarding his cut. The kid then looked at me and apologized for cutting into my time. I told him no worries—I felt bad for the kid. He went to another coach and showed him the cut. Coach Steve was watching this kid from the ring and shaking his head in disgust and said, "Look at him. He's a mama's boy. He's soft!" I said, "No disrespect, Coach, but aren't you being hard on the kid?"

Coach Steve went from intensely watching this kid from the ring to having his focus on me. "Oh shit," I thought. This was getting real. Coach Steve then said, "Why are you here?" I started to stutter with my response. The last thing I wanted to do was insult this guy. He then said to me, "You're a corporate guy, right? Martial arts is like a hobby for you, right?" I said yes. He looked at me and said, "That's cool. I get that, and I respect that. But you see that motherfucker sitting on the bench with a scared look on his face?" I said "Yes."

Steve continued with his speech: "That kid just came to Vegas a month ago to become a fighter. He drove from Chicago and left his family and friends to become a fighter. Look how he reacted over a little cut on his face. He completely shut down and panicked. The cut was small, no damage at all. What's going to happen to him when he gets half his face split open from a punch, knee, or elbow? What's going to happen then? He doesn't have what it takes to be a fighter. He doesn't have the heart to be a fighter. The best thing I can do is tell that kid to go back home and not to waste the prime of his life chasing something that will never happen and that can possibly hurt him really bad."

Coach Steve then began to break it down more for me. He said that people are born fighters, that it's something you either have or don't. That some people are born tough and have a high pain tolerance, a warrior's heart. "I seen the fight game ruin a lot of people. It's a hard life. I want to help this kid and prevent him from getting seriously hurt and getting a broken spirit. He doesn't have what it takes—that's why I'm hard on him. You dig?" he said. I responded, "I dig."

I was completely taken aback by the brilliant breakdown of what just transpired. Coach Steve went deep, rabbit hole deep, with me. I just looked at him and said, "WOW." Coach Steve said, "OK, let's get back to work." After the lesson, Coach Steve said I had good blocks and parries and that we would cover more the next day.

My next lesson was with Coach Dan. I had a half-hour to rest up before my Muay Thai kickboxing lesson. Coach Steve told me that Coach Dan was one of the best fighters he had ever seen but was forced to retire because of recurring hand injuries. Finally, my time arrived to train with Coach Dan. He was soft-spoken, but after hearing about him and watching him train, I knew he was a serious fighter and martial artist. There was a group of fighters just sitting on the side, watching me train with him. The first thing he wanted me to do was shadow-box. I was self-conscious about doing this in front of real fighters. I was getting worked up, overwhelmed with anxiety, but then I just cleared my mind. I just blocked it all out and continued to punch and kick. It took a lot of nerve, but I was glad that I did it. It was all in my head; I knew because the fighters were really cool and friendly to me, and I think they respected me for just keeping it real and doing what came natural to me, right or wrong.

It was extremely humbling to shadow-box in front of real fighters who ate and paid bills with fighting. Coach Dan had his own style, much different from Coach Steve's. He was showing me how to up my kicking game. After training, we talked about workout plans and diet. In a nice way, Dan was telling me that I needed to lose some weight. He mentioned how it was important to eat every two hours. It was quite evident that he took his job seriously. Coach Dan began to break down my game plan and what I needed to work on. He suggested that I lose some weight to become faster. He also said the same thing that Coach Steve had—that I fought too close and stayed in close range too long. That I needed to get in and out.

When I was done with both lessons, I was tired, sore, and inspired. When I got to my room, I began to journal my experiences from the lessons. I catalogued by thoughts, feelings, and connections I made with technique and how it was taught as well as details about my interactions with the coaches. The next day for training, I was less nervous and more excited. It was the same schedule as the day before: hands first and then Muay Thai. Coach Dan's first words to me were that he was going to kill me in training with today's lessons. By the time I was done, I was exhausted and thanked both trainers for the lessons and insight. While I was there, I met a lot of cool fighters, very down to earth. A lot of them admired that I just came to Vegas to take lessons and learn. I was more fascinated to hear their stories. Some had left their homes young to pursue their dreams of becoming champion fighters. All these cats seemed to be on a different level than I was; their commitment and discipline to eat and train was unlike anything I had ever seen. Their lives seemed to revolve around training and fighting.

Just watching these guys train and spar freaked me out. I had never seen that type of sparring live. They were all so talented in all aspects of combat. They all seemed to possess superb boxing, kicking, wrestling, and jujitsu skills. I saw one kid get picked up and slammed to the floor. He had troubled breathing, and the match was over. But what impressed me most was that after he recovered, he went back to practice and was training like nothing had ever happened to him. His head was in the game.

Humbled as I was, a few of the fighters gave me some props on my game while they saw me training. I was taken aback by that because there were times when I felt exhausted and had low energy to continue the practice. Then one of the fighters patted me on the back and said, "Keep going, bro!" That meant a lot to me. Here was a real fighter training for his next fight, and he was encouraging a wannabe fighter.

Overall, the experience I got from training in Vegas was much more than I had expected. It was deeper than just technique. The takeaway was that there are fighters who are martial artists and hobbyists who are martial artists. I'm a hobbyist. I enjoy learning martial arts and boxing for a creative outlet and self-defense, and every now and then, I will spar with headgear. That's as far as I want to take it. Watching these fighters spar and train live was a major lesson for me. These fighters had superpower fighting skills but still remained down to earth. It made me think of some of the martial artists and boxers back home I'd met along my journey and how shallow and stuck-up some were. They were at nowhere near the levels of these fighters. A lot of people I have known and met think they're hot shit, but if they trained at this gym, they would be humbled very quickly.

Many people call themselves fighters; even I do. But after that experience, I'm careful when I use the word "fighter" in martial arts. I'm a fighter in life, love, honor, family, and business. But in martial arts, I'm a hobbyist. In self-defense, I'm prepared to defend myself. But even shadow-boxing in front of real professional fighters for three minutes seemed like an hour. But I did it. I kept my focus tight and blocked everything out. I didn't focus on what they thought of my skills or my shadow-boxing. I kept it real and did it my way regardless of what people thought of my skill. What's important is that I finished it. And finally, the biggest takeaway for me is when Coach Steve broke it down for me about that kid in the ring. How he panicked and just shut down. It takes a lot to be a fighter, more mental than physical. Everybody has a different pain tolerance, and most fighters have a high one. They can take more punishment than the average person. Coach Steve taught me how important it is to have heart. Listening to him tell me, "That kid doesn't have what it takes to be a fighter; he needs to pack his bags and go back home," changed me. Coach Steve brought me into a painful reality on how hard and brutal the fighting world is. After seeing that, I knew I'd gotten my money's worth, and everything I learned after that was gravy.

Going to Vegas for training was a rush for me—an epic moment. And to this day, I continue to travel to the West Coast, sometimes twice per year. It's become a ritual for me to go to California and Vegas for training. I strongly recommend it. Do it! The amount of insight and skill you will learn is remarkable.

Chapter 12: Haters, Bullies, and Fake People: The Sword and Shield Concept

"**Don't** let negative and toxic people rent space in your head. Raise the rent and kick them out!"
—Robert Tew

I once heard that behind every successful person, there is a busload of haters looking to destroy that person. Haters are everywhere, and when you lose one, there are five more ready to take that hater's place. On my journey, I have come across all kinds of haters, both in my personal work and my martial arts journey. The major underlying motive that drives your haters to hate is massive envy toward their targets. I'm not a hater, though at times I can get full of envy toward someone, especially the person who always comes out on top and lets you know it. Instead of hating, I force myself to try to learn from the experience what makes someone win. Some people will just hate for various reasons. I like to follow the golden-rule approach. Treat people the way you want to be treated. Be real, be humble, and be brave. If someone doesn't like you just because of the way you look, talk, or walk, that's their problem and not yours. Your mind is free and strong, and their mind is full of fear, anger, and weakness.

As I got older, I came up with a game/technique that has now become a habit for me. I learned how to protect my mind from haters and their negative feedback. This came to me while I was watching the movie *300*. It was the part when the Persians shot all those arrows toward the Spartans. The Spartans banded together and put their shields up and blocked all of the arrows. Then, after the rain of arrows was over, King Leonidas got up, took his sword, and cut the arrows that were stuck in his shield. That was an epic scene for me. It got me thinking about training my mind to protect myself from negative people and feedback so that I would know what to do when I came across a hater who was trying to corrupt my mind with toxic words. I think of it as a massive poisonous arrow attack on my mind. Then my mind becomes like Spartan warriors that band together and lift their shields to block the poison-tipped arrows intended to destroy my mind and spirit.

It took me some time and practice, but I'm getting more effective at dealing with haters. It has worked wonders for me. The ability to have faith in yourself and not allow toxic people to contaminate your head and have their negative words mass-produce like fleas and ticks in your head has helped me preserve my power and confidence. Sometimes, people who are trying to help you might come across as haters. Listen to what they are trying to tell you. Ask yourself, "Will this help me? Or is this negative bullshit or useless information that serves no positive purpose?" If that's the case, then just block with your shield and move on. I think we all have been bullied at some point in our lives, and some of us may have been bullies ourselves. I'm no expert, but from what I've read and heard on the news, some kids are bullied so bad physically and mentally that they commit suicide. It just breaks my heart. If you're a kid in school and ever feel overwhelmed from bullying, reach out for help. Talk to a parent, guardian, family member, friend, teacher, or member of the police. There are people out there who can help you—always remember that! If you're getting bullied, you should learn how to defend yourself and stick up for yourself. It takes a lot of courage, hard work, and dedication. But in time, you will see it's the best thing you can do for yourself. Search for schools, and do your research. Let an instructor know that you need help.

Tell them, "I'm getting bullied, and I need to learn some skills ASAP!" If you're having money issues and can't afford lessons, check out YouTube. There are plenty of good self-defense videos on there. Also, inquire to see whether there are any free self-defense courses in your community. Always do your research, and make sure it's legit, and you're learning in a safe environment. Or if you're old enough, get a part-time job so that you can pay for your own lessons. Remember that there will always be a door that leads to a new path on your journey. I have seen bullies in all areas of my journey, in my job and even in the martial arts. The more you train, the better you are with dealing with these low self-esteem individuals. Sometimes, you have to stand up to your bullies, and sometimes it doesn't matter whether you win or lose. I know we all want to win, but there is always the possibility that you will lose a fight. But always remember that what's important is you showed heart and honor and stood your ground. It takes a lot of guts and courage to stand up to a bully. But with the right training over time, you will see that you have the skills to rise to the occasion. People will say that this kid is no joke, that he or she does not mess around. They will throw down for their honor and respect.

Over the years, I have learned to view my training as my sword and shield. I hear my sword strike, and I hear my shield defend. I use this concept when dealing with problems in life, both physical and mental. Fighting should always be your last option. But if you're in a situation where you feel threatened and can't flee, then you must defend yourself. Now for dealing with fake people, there is really no cure. Fake people are in all aspects of life. I have just learned to take people for what they are and see where the chips fall. I have never really fit in. I have always marched to the beat of my own drum. Sometimes, I feel like I'm an old soul from another generation because I believe that honor, respect, and your word should mean something. Nowadays, it seems that a lot of people don't care about those things. They will lie to your face with no remorse. It's all about them and nobody else. I strongly reject that school of thought, and I do not allow people who have that mindset into my personal circle. At work and even at training, I must learn how to work with people like this—I have no choice. It took me a long time to come to this realization.

When people talk about other people behind their backs and try to destroy their character and reputations but are nice to their face and give fake smiles, it makes me sick. It's not honorable. But as I've gotten older, I have learned to accept that it's a way of life. That is who they really are. It was from my martial arts journey that I developed a strong, confident mind to stand alone and at times hold my own hand. Through my training, I learned what true strength and confidence are. You reach a point when you no longer care what people think of you. Does a lion care what a sheep thinks of him? No. I learned to stay focused on my goal and what I want to accomplish—not to take my eyes off the target.

An unknown author wisely said, "Feed your focus and starve your distractions." You must be strong and have laser-like focus so that nothing can break your will and motivation. That's power! Negative opinions from others begin to lose their sting and have little effect. I burn them as fuel for my journey. Sometimes, this negative feedback can be an opportunity to improve your craft in all aspects of life. The trick is what to focus on. My sword and shield help me strike down and block out all the bullshit, and they get me to the heart of what really matters—I can tell what's important and what's not important. Martial arts have made me very strong. They have given me one of the greatest gifts, mental endurance. This has allowed me to endure and remain positive and persistent in achieving my goals. Sometimes it takes a while, but no matter what, I keep on training.

Chapter 13: No Regrets—Thanks for Taking the Ride with Me

"But when you walk **your own path** in life, others will be irritated and often offended. That's their problem, not yours."
—Chris McCombs

At the end of 2014, I had to make a tough decision regarding my JKD training. Because of my work hours, how far I lived away from the dojo, and the wear and tear on my car, I decided to cancel my membership temporarily. It had been difficult for me to make class. I couldn't see wasting my money and paying for something that I couldn't enjoy. I will be back one day. I have been training there since 2005—almost ten years of great memories, life lessons, and personal accomplishments. But I had to make a business decision. JKD was and still is the martial art for me. It fit me and accepted me.

These days, I do a lot of training at home. I practice a lot of punching and kicking. I do many reps in front of the mirror, just mastering the basics. I also do a lot of shadow-boxing, visualizing my opponent or opponents attacking me from all ranges and angles. I view shadow-boxing as doing a kata, and it takes years to get good and understand it. You can tell whether someone is good at shadow-boxing. If you closely watch people who do it well, you can almost see the imaginary opponent they're sparring. They go deep in their mind, reacting to this make-believe fight. With all the traveling I did and all the different boxing and MMA gyms I trained at, I learned that many fighters take shadow-boxing seriously and feel it's a skill that takes years to develop and understand. Some fighters have told me that they reached a mental state in which they really felt that they were fighting someone.

As far as jumping rope goes, I still do it. I jump three times per week for seven minutes straight. I don't do it every day; I scaled down a little bit. Over the years, I've put some wear and tear on my joints, especially my knees, but it was all worth it. I still jump and move well. Jumping rope has done wonders for me as a martial artist. It is great for cardio, develops good footwork, and strengthens your focus and mental endurance to help you push through the pain and keep moving forward. I also still get in some mitt work every few months, not to mention my annual trips to California and Vegas for private lessons with well-known martial artists. I'm still working on my game. I've been doing these trips now for seven years. No matter who I train with, the instructors stress the importance of solo training at home to master the basics. Constant drilling over and over again. Some of my best lessons have occurred during talks I have had with these teachers or fighters about their daily routines and what keeps them up to speed on their training as well as their personal philosophies on life and training. Whenever I travel, I feel like a wandering ninja looking to build on my game. I just roll with it, trusting my blind faith.

Last year, I started going to mindfulness meditation class when I had the time. I'm really digging it. I'm learning how to clear my mind and control my thoughts to have no attachment—just to observe and use my breath as a focal point. Some of this I already knew instinctually or from reading and talking with other martial artists along my journey. It made me feel good to discover that all these years I have been meditating without even knowing it. I try to meditate fifteen minutes per day to help keep me relaxed. Every time I meditate, I'm giving my mind a relaxing shampoo after a long, hard day of work and training. It still bothers me I'm not training at the JKD school, but I continue to practice at home. So many martial arts books I've read over the years mention that many martial artists brought their skill sets to the next level through solo training.

Sometimes on your journey in martial arts and in life, you must make difficult decisions. For example, you may reach a point in your training where you outgrow your dojo or your dojo outgrows you. Maybe you lose interest or don't like some of the people you train with. It happens; it's part of the journey. But always remember that there are new roads and paths that will lead you in different directions and on new adventures. The key is to always be training and learning. We all start out as white belts, but the older I get and the more training and different experiences I go through, the more I believe we will always be white belts. From the bottom of my heart, I strongly believe that this mindset keeps one growing and evolving as a martial artist and successful person. To be free from ego and self-imposed limitations is a lifelong process. Every now and then, we need to kill our egos and put the white belt back on.

Well, that's all, folks. Thanks for taking the ride with me. Remember, I'm no martial arts expert or fighter. I'm a just a regular dude who enjoys training in martial arts as a hobby. I'm a champ in my own life. Martial arts were a huge driving factor for me. If I had to sum up my experiences in one sentence, it would be: "Fall, stand, and repeat." It's through all the standing up in and falling from different moments in my life that I discovered who I am and what I am made of. I had to resolve to rise back and stand my ground with confidence, faith, and purpose. Again, I'm just an average dude with average martial arts skills, nothing crazy. Martial arts have been my powerful engine all throughout my life and have helped me through dark and stormy times while I was doing incredible things that I never thought I would accomplish.

I have good days, and I have bad days. But for whatever reason, I always choose to focus on the positive side of the situation. All people have a moment in their lives when something clicks and they find out what they love to do. For me, that moment was when my father trained me that summer for the Taekwondo Junior Olympics. He introduced me to jump rope, prepared me with sprints and jumping on milk crates, and worked on my punching and kicking combos. The end result is that I won a silver medal at ten years old. The hard work and trust that my father instilled in me—to have faith in my technique—helped me on my lifelong journey as a martial artist. When shit gets bad and things go wrong, I just remember that I won a silver medal.

I used to get sad when I realized I would never physically have the silver medal to hold in my hands because my Taekwondo instructor lost it, but I think never possessing it kept me on this journey. It was meant to be that I never physically got it. Who knows . . . maybe if I did have it, I would have stopped my training in the martial arts. That would have been my tombstone. So, I have no regrets. Down the road, I think I would like to open my own school and teach martial arts with a strong emphasis on self-defense and developing a strong, positive mental attitude to promote healthy mind, body, and spirit.

I hope this book inspires you and motivates you to continue, go back, or start your martial arts journey. Thank you for your time.

About Anthony Vano

Anthony Vano is a Martial Artist with over 20 years of experience in self-defense. He's an NLP practitioner, Motivator and a strong believer in having a positive mental attitude.

Readers may contact the author via email: fallstandrepeat@aol.com

CPSIA information can be obtained
at www.ICGtesting.com
Printed in the USA
FFOW03n1015060318
45440726-46156FF